NUTRITION & HEALTH

Food Myths and Facts

ADAM WOOG

LUCENT BOOKS

A part of Gale, Cengage Learning

Detroit • New York • San Francisco • New Haven, Conn • Waterville, Maine • London

LIBRARY OF CONGRESS CATALOGING-IN-PUBLICATION DATA

Woog, Adam, 1953-
    Food myths and facts / by Adam Woog.
        p. cm. -- (Nutrition and health)
    Includes bibliographical references and index.
    ISBN 978-1-4205-0270-1 (hardcover)
    1. Nutrition--Popular works. I. Title.
    RA784.W66 2011
    613.2--dc22

                                                    2010035960

Lucent Books
27500 Drake Rd.
Farmington Hills, MI 48331

ISBN-13: 978-1-4205-0270-1
ISBN-10: 1-4205-0270-0

Printed in the United States of America
1 2 3 4 5 6 7 14 13 12 11 10

Printed by Bang Printing, Brainerd, MN, 1st Ptg., 01/2011

TABLE OF CONTENTS

FOREWORD

Many people today are often amazed by the amount of nutrition and health information, often contradictory, that can be found in the media. Television, newspapers, and magazines bombard readers with the latest news and recommendations. Television news programs report on recent scientific studies. The healthy living sections of newspapers and magazines offer information and advice. In addition, electronic media such as websites, blogs, and forums post daily nutrition and health news and recommendations.

This constant stream of information can be confusing. The science behind nutrition and health is constantly evolving. Current research often leads to new ideas and insights. Many times, the latest nutrition studies and health recommendations contradict previous studies or traditional health advice. When the media report these changes without giving context or explanations, consumers become confused. In a survey by the National Health Council, for example, 68 percent of participants agreed that "when reporting medical and health news, the media often contradict themselves, so I don't know what to believe." In addition, the Food Marketing Institute reported that eight out of ten consumers thought it was likely that nutrition and health experts would have a completely different idea about what foods are healthy within five years. With so much contradictory information, people have difficulty deciding how to apply nutrition and health recommendations to their lives. Students find it difficult to find relevant yet clear and credible information for reports.

Changing recommendations for antioxidant supplements are an example of how confusion can arise. In the 1990s antioxidants, such as vitamins C and E and beta-carotene, came to the public's attention. Scientists found that people who ate more antioxidant-rich foods had a lower risk of heart disease, cancer, vision loss, and other chronic conditions than those who ate lower amounts. Without waiting for more scientific study, the media and supplement companies quickly spread the word that antioxidants could help fight and prevent disease. They recommended that people take antioxidant supplements and eat fortified foods. When further scientific studies were completed, however, most did not support the initial recommendations. While naturally occurring antioxidants in fruits and vegetables may help prevent a variety of chronic diseases, little scientific evidence proved antioxidant supplements had the same effect. In fact, a study published in the November 2008 *Journal of the American Medical Association* found that supplemental vitamins A and C gave no more heart protection than a placebo. The study's results contradicted the widely publicized recommendation, leading to consumer confusion. This example highlights the importance of context for evaluating nutrition and health news. Understanding a topic's scientific background, interpreting a study's findings, and evaluating news sources are critical skills that help reduce confusion.

Lucent's Nutrition and Health series is designed to help young people sift through the mountain of confusing facts, opinions, and recommendations. Each book contains the most up-to-date information, synthesized and written so that students can understand and think critically about nutrition and health issues. Each volume of the series provides a balanced overview of today's hot-button nutrition and health issues while presenting the latest scientific findings and a discussion of issues surrounding the topic. The series provides young people with tools for evaluating conflicting and ever-changing ideas about nutrition and health. Clear narrative peppered with personal anecdotes, fully documented primary and secondary source quotes, informative sidebars, fact boxes, and statistics are all used to help readers understand these topics and how they affect their bodies and their lives. Each volume includes information about changes in trends over time, political controversies, and international perspectives. Full-color photographs and charts enhance all volumes in the series. The Nutrition and Health series is a valuable resource for young people to understand current topics and make informed choices for themselves.

Sifting Out the Truth

Everybody needs food. People love to talk about it, and people love to consume it—sometimes to the point of obsession. Sharing a meal has always been an important social and cultural aspect of human society. Eating certain foods can also contribute to better health.

Naturally, a topic as important, broad, and interesting as nutrition leads to endless theories about what combination of food and exercise is necessary to maintain optimum health. Some theories make sense, some are dubious, and others are just wrong. In fact, one of the lasting truths about diet is that a lot of information is available. The sad fact is that wrong information about what to eat is rampant.

Worse, it sometimes seems as though experts keep changing their minds. At one time, for instance, health researchers announced that eating eggs could contribute significantly to heart disease. Further research has since indicated, however, that for the majority of people, eggs are not as unhealthy as once believed.

As new information about food develops, new theories emerge about what exactly constitutes the best diet for optimum health. Some of these theories are supported by solid research and scientific studies. Others are not. Although research does not guarantee the truth or falsehood of a theory, a properly conducted study can be a strong indicator that a given topic is either myth or reality.

Mountains of Information

With so much information and so many conflicting ideas, deciding what to believe can be tough. Furthermore, separating truth from myth becomes more complex daily. Thanks to the Internet, rumors and false information can spread quickly—much faster than serious scientific research can prove or disprove them.

In the middle of all the available information, however, a few basic truths remain. Here is one: The best nutrition is a variety of fresh and healthy food. Here is another: The simple rule behind losing weight is to eat fewer calories than are used. Yet as anyone struggling to lose weight knows, just because something is simple does not necessarily mean it is easy.

Understanding the role that nutrition plays in health can be helpful in minimizing the problems posed by a score of

The best diet contains an assortment of fresh and nutritious foods.

diseases. For example, overeating leads to obesity, and obesity is reaching epidemic proportions in America, not just among adults but among teens and children as well. Obesity, in turn, can raise a person's risk for a host of health problems, including diabetes, stroke, and heart disease. Getting a firm understanding of the facts involved in the relationship between food and health provides a basis for making smart nutritional choices.

Before sifting through the mountains of information about nutrition and separating myths from facts, it is important to understand some of the basics about how the body uses food. Knowing the fundamentals of nutrition helps in making smart choices about food.

CHAPTER 1

Nutrition 101

K nowing the fundamentals of nutrition is an important part of understanding how food affects health. All foods contain varying amounts of nutrients. Some of these nutrients are classified as vitamins, such as vitamin A, vitamin B, and vitamin D, and others are considered minerals, such as calcium, potassium, and iron. Still others are naturally occurring chemicals and substances, notably calories, protein, cholesterol, carbohydrates, fats, and fiber.

To determine which foods to eat for maximum benefit, it is helpful to organize foods into different groups since different foods provide different nutritional values. The best-known set of organized food groups are those in the nutrition guide known as MyPyramid, created by the U.S. government.

Climbing the Pyramid

MyPyramid, sometimes informally called the food pyramid, is written and updated by the U.S. Department of Agriculture. This nutrition guide provides recommendations about what kinds of nutrition are best for a healthy lifestyle. It gives tips on how much of each kind of food is ideal, depending on such individual factors as size, gender, age, and exercise level. MyPyramid also recommends the amount of calories that should be consumed. A calorie is a measure of heat. Calories measure how much energy the body gets from food and how efficiently it burns that energy. MyPyramid recommends a diet that provides a total of two thousand calories a day for moderately active female teens and twenty-eight hundred for moderately active male teens. The numbers are generally a little lower for adults.

The Food Groups

MyPyramid organizes food into basic groups. The groups are grains, vegetables, fruits, oils, dairy, and legumes and meats. The literature and website for MyPyramid feature an image of a multicolored pyramid that illustrates the importance of each of these groups. Each group is color

The major food groups are grains, vegetables, fruits, oils, dairy, and legumes and meat.

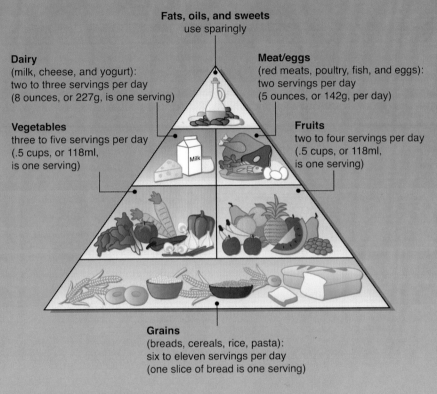

The Food Guide Pyramid

The U.S. Department of Agriculture recommends the following servings per day for teens and adults:

Fats, oils, and sweets
use sparingly

Dairy
(milk, cheese, and yogurt):
two to three servings per day
(8 ounces, or 227g, is one serving)

Meat/eggs
(red meats, poultry, fish, and eggs):
two servings per day
(5 ounces, or 142g, per day)

Vegetables
three to five servings per day
(.5 cups, or 118ml,
is one serving)

Fruits
two to four servings per day
(.5 cups, or 118ml,
is one serving)

Grains
(breads, cereals, rice, pasta):
six to eleven servings per day
(one slice of bread is one serving)

Taken from: USDA Food and Nutrition Service, "Pyramid Servings: How Much? How Many?"
www.fns.usda.gov/tn/Resources/nibbles/pyramid_servings.pdf.

coded: orange for grains, green for vegetables, red for fruits, yellow for oils, blue for dairy, and purple for legumes and meats. Climbing a set of stairs on one side of the pyramid is a human figure, representing the importance of combining exercise with a healthy eating plan.

Grains

Among the most common kinds of grain are rice, wheat, oats, barley, and bran. Cereal, bread, pasta, and crackers are made from grains. Some grain-based foods are made with whole grains, which have been minimally processed and generally have more nutritional value. MyPyramid recommends six daily servings of grains. One serving (also called an ounce equivalent) of grain is about one slice of bread; 0.5 cup (118ml) of cooked rice, pasta, or cereal; or 1 ounce (28g) of cold cereal. At least half of these portions should be whole grains.

Vegetables and Fruits

Vegetables are naturally low in fat and calories, so they are good for weight loss and general health. Vegetables also provide fiber, which aids in digestion, as well as a wide range of vitamins and minerals. MyPyramid recommends five servings daily from the vegetable group, about 2.5 cups (591ml) total. One serving is about 0.5 cup (118ml) of raw or cooked vegetables, 0.5 cup (118ml) vegetable juice, or 1 cup (237ml) of leafy raw vegetables. For example, one serving size of broccoli is about as big as a standard-size lightbulb. One serving size of potato is about as big as a computer mouse.

Like vegetables, fruits are low in fat. They are also rich in natural sugars, fiber, and other nutrients. Because variety and freshness are important in getting the most out of fruit and vegetables, a mix of fresh produce is best. Yet canned, frozen, and dried fruits and vegetables can substitute if necessary.

According to MyPyramid, two to four servings of fruit, about 1 to 2 cups (237ml to 473ml), should be included in a daily diet. One serving size of fruit is generally about as big as a tennis ball. The specific vegetables and fruits that are best depend on an individual's needs. For example, if a person is in need of vitamin A, cantaloupes, peaches, oranges, and blackberries are especially rich in it.

NUTRITION FACT

Less than 10 percent

Number of U.S. high school students who get MyPyramid's recommended three servings of vegetables and two servings of fruits each day

Oils

Oils are fats that are liquid at room temperature, notably oils used for cooking, such as olive oil and canola oil. There

How Many Calories a Day?

Everyone knows that too many calories, usually from fatty or sugary foods, can lead to obesity and other serious health problems. Yet not everyone knows just how many calories they need each day. The body uses a lot of calories just to maintain its basic functions (breathing, pumping the heart, and so on), so a basic minimum is always necessary. The body burns large amounts of calories during exercise and the movements of daily living. Finding the right calorie level can be tricky.

Daily minimums vary for the calories and nutrients needed to keep the metabolism in good working order. Among the factors are age, gender, height, body type, and activity level. The Riley Hospital for Children in Indianapolis, Indiana, recommends that active boys aged fifteen through eighteen should consume three thousand calories per day while getting fifty-nine grams of protein, twelve milligrams of iron, fifteen milligrams of zinc, and thirteen hundred milligrams of calcium. For active girls in the same age range, the hospital recommends that they consume a total of twenty-two hundred calories per day and get forty-four grams of protein, fifteen milligrams of iron, twelve milligrams of zinc, and thirteen hundred milligrams of calcium.

Riley Hospital for Children, "Adolescents: 12–21." http://rileychildrens hospital.com/parents-and-patients/caring-for-kids/adolescents.jsp.

is also oil in food that has a fairly high fat content, such as nuts, avocados, mayonnaise, and soft margarine. Fats that are solid at room temperature, such as butter, are known simply as solid fats. These are primarily the fats found in meat. A certain amount of fat is necessary for good health, but only a small amount is needed. Teenage girls need only five teaspoons of fats or oils per day, and teenage boys need only six. Most Americans get enough oils from the foods they eat every day.

Dairy

Dairy food comes from the milk of certain animals, mainly cows and goats. Milk, yogurt, butter, and cheese are the most common kinds of dairy. Dairy is high in calcium, which the body needs for bone strength, and also contains proteins, vitamins, and minerals. Dairy can be high in fat, however, so low-fat or nonfat versions are best. As a general rule, many nutritionists recommend one thousand milligrams of calcium a day, a level that can be reached with three servings of dairy. Three servings is roughly equivalent to 3 cups (710ml) of milk or yogurt, or 6 ounces (170g) of cheese.

Legumes and Meats

The legumes and meat food group includes legumes, meat, nuts, and seeds. Legumes are beans and peas, such as lentils, chickpeas, and kidney beans. Legumes are low in fat, high in fiber, and contain a variety of other nutrients the body needs. Meat includes meat from animals, eggs, and fish—all rich sources of protein. Not many portions of these foods are needed on a daily basis. MyPyramid recommends 5.5 servings a day. One serving equals 1 ounce (28g) of poultry, fish, or cooked beans; one egg; one tablespoon of peanut butter; or 0.5 ounce (14g) of nuts or seeds. This is a much smaller amount of protein than most Americans eat. For instance, 3 ounces (85g) of cooked lean meat, a good amount for an average adult or teen to eat at one meal (and providing about half of the daily recommended protein), is about the size of a deck of cards. For people who do not eat meat, good sources of protein include legumes and soy-based foods like tofu.

To determine which combination of foods to eat for maximum benefit, it is necessary to think smaller—down to the molecular level, in fact. This is because it is within the body's cells that nutrients do their job.

Proteins and Carbohydrates

Consuming the right amounts of protein, carbohydrates, and fats is essential for good health. All three are sources of energy for the body. Proteins are naturally occurring chemicals. In terms of nutrition, proteins are calorie sources that are essential to building and maintaining bones, muscles, organs, and other parts of the body. They help the body recover from injury and disease, build red blood cells, and otherwise keep it alive and healthy. Without enough protein, the body may experience loss of muscle mass, decreased immunity to disease, a weakening of the heart and respiratory systems, and, in extreme cases, death.

Carbohydrates (carbs) are also calorie sources that provide energy. Carbs are grouped into two categories: complex and simple. Abundant quantities of complex carbs are found in food that is high in an energy store called starch, such as potatoes, pasta, oats, and legumes. The body breaks down these complex carbs into a blood sugar called glucose, which it then uses as a source for caloric energy. Complex

Complex carbohydrates supply the body with its main sources of energy. They are, from left, oats, bread, potato, rice, pasta, and wheat.

carbs provide the bulk of the body's long-lasting energy, and nutritionists recommend that they should be about half of the calories consumed each day.

Simple carbs are absorbed in the body faster than complex carbs. Simple carbs include the refined sugars found in candy, soda, and table sugar. Because they break down in the body quickly, they supply a fast burst of energy. Yet they provide little else in terms of nutrition. This is why simple carbs are called empty calories.

Good Fats vs. Bad Fats

The third source of energy for the body, after proteins and carbohydrates, is fat. Nuts, meat, dairy products, and eggs are common sources of fat. A common misconception is that fats should be avoided, but this is not entirely true. Too much fat is a problem in terms of weight control and disease, but fat is still an essential part of nutrition. Besides giving the body energy, fat helps it absorb nutrients, keeps nerve transmissions and cell membranes in good working order, and performs other useful functions. If genuinely starving, the body draws on stored fat to keep itself alive.

Although some fat is beneficial to nutrition, it is important not to rely too heavily on fats for energy. Some experts suggest that only about 25 to 35 percent of food calories should come from fats. Other experts say the percentage should be even lower.

An important distinction to make is between so-called good fats (monounsaturated fats and, to a lesser degree, polyunsaturated fats) and bad fats (trans and saturated fats). Fat is a source of cholesterol, a waxy substance in the blood and cells of the body. Cholesterol helps maintain cell membranes and do other jobs, so a certain amount is needed. Too much cholesterol, however, clogs the body's arteries and dramatically raises the risk of heart disease, strokes, and other serious problems.

Good fats are found in food that comes primarily from plants, such as olive, flax, soybean, sunflower, peanut, canola, and corn oils. Olive oil is the oil of choice for many nutritionists because it is primarily monounsaturated and less processed.

Nutrition Facts

Serving Size 2 Cakes/1 Pkg (60g)
Servings Per Container 6

Amount Per Serving

Calories 220   Calories from Fat 70

	% Daily Value*
Total Fat 7g	11%
Saturated Fat 2.5g	13%
Trans Fat 0g	
Cholesterol 10mg	3%
Sodium 270mg	11%
Total Carbohydrate 36g	12%
Dietary Fiber 2g	7%
Sugars 27g	
Protein 2g	

Nutrition labels specify how many grams of the so-called bad fats— saturated and trans fats—a product has in order to help consumers make an informed choice about the food they eat.

Among the kinds of food with high amounts of bad fats are manufactured fats, such as solid vegetable shortening. The same is true for fats that have been altered by overuse or over-heating, like those often found in commercial fryers used to make deep-fried foods. These altered fats (trans fats) are wide-ly considered the most damaging to health. Many nutritionists and doctors also suggest limiting the intake of the saturated fat found in animal products, such as meat and dairy.

Fiber

Another important nutritional building block is fiber. Fiber (sometimes called roughage or bulk) is the part of food from plants that the body does not digest completely. Instead, the body excretes it fairly quickly. Still, fiber is important, notably because it aids in preventing digestive problems. Some evidence also supports the idea that fiber may help prevent heart disease, gastrointestinal problems, and diabetes. Most Americans get far too little of it. An easy way to tell if enough fiber is being eaten is if bowel movements are soft and easy to pass. The opposite is true when the body takes in too little fiber.

Fiber is classified in two ways: as soluble (able to dissolve in water) or insoluble (unable to dissolve in water). Both are essential for good health. Foods such as oatmeal, beans, peas, rice, bran, barley, citrus fruits, strawberries, and apple pulp contain large amounts of soluble fiber. Good sources for insoluble fiber include most grains, cabbage, beets, carrots, brussel sprouts, turnips, cauliflower, and apple skin. MyPyramid recommends a total daily intake of at least 28 grams of dietary fiber. This can be found in roughly 2.5 cups (591ml) of raw or cooked vegetables or six slices of whole-grain bread.

The Basics of Vitamins and Minerals

Foods contain various vitamins and minerals, another major category of nutrients. Vitamins are organic substances that are identified by letter: vitamin A, vitamin B, vitamin C, and so on. Minerals, meanwhile, are inorganic chemicals such as iron, zinc, and potassium. Both vitamins and minerals are essential for good nutrition. Both are found, in different amounts, in various kinds of food, as well as in dietary supplements, such as ginseng root, garlic, flaxseed oil, and cod-liver oil.

In theory, a person should be able to get all the nutrients needed for health just from food. Yet in reality, this is not often the case. Getting the right amount from food alone can be very difficult, in part because it can be hard to find enough healthy, fresh food, and not everyone is willing to eat (or can afford) only high-quality food. It is thus often the case that people need extra vitamins and minerals, and they obtain them by consuming them in pill form. It is currently unknown, however, if synthetically manufactured vitamins are as effective as those found naturally in food, and the issue is hotly debated by strong advocates on both sides. Some nutritionists believe that synthetic vitamins are not even close to being as effective as natural ones. They argue that, among other factors, natural vitamins and minerals are absorbed much more completely. On the other hand, many experts assert that there is no definitive proof that the body can even tell the difference between synthetic vitamins and those that come directly from natural sources.

The fact remains, however, that supplements alone do not provide enough of the vitamins, minerals, and other nutrients that the body needs. They are important additions to an overall eating plan, not a complete solution. Food provides nutrients that not even the best supplements can provide, such as fiber, protein, carbohydrates, and fat. Without these components of an overall eating plan, vitamins are only partially useful. Carol Haggans, a nutrition consultant with the National Institutes of Health, comments, "People shouldn't feel they can make up for an unhealthy diet by taking a multivitamin-mineral supplement."[1]

Recommended Daily Intake Values

Relying on the recommended daily intake (RDI) values that are found on vitamin labels may not always be enough. For one thing, the needs of individuals for specific vitamins and minerals can vary widely. Also, there is considerable disagreement about what the optimum levels for these nutritional supplements might be.

For example, many nutritionists say that the U.S. government's RDI of vitamin D, four hundred international units, is too low. One expert who agrees with this assessment is Susan Harris of the U.S. Department of Agriculture's Jean Mayer Human Nutrition Research Center on Aging at Tufts University in Boston, Massachusetts. She comments,

> Not getting enough vitamin D is common, particularly in the winter, when, in the northern U.S., [our bodies] don't make it from the sun. Almost everyone working in this field agrees that the vitamin D recommendations are too low. Many people are well below where they should be and don't know it. It's easy to remedy with a vitamin D supplement, but a multivitamin isn't enough.

Quoted in Center for Science in the Public Interest, "Surprise! Ten Myths That Can Trip You Up," The Free Library, 2008, www.thefreelibrary.com/surprise!+ten+myths+that+can+trip+you+up.-a0175548096.

Supplements for vitamins A, B, C, D, and E are sold in large quantities, but a debate rages about whether they are as effective as the vitamins found in foods.

Essential Vitamins

Certain vitamins and minerals are considered essential for good health. If the body lacks these, health problems can result. In extreme cases, a lack of certain vitamins and minerals can endanger health permanently. One of the most important vitamins is vitamin A. It keeps skin, eyesight, and digestive and urinary tracts at their best. Too little vitamin A can result in dry or flaky skin, loss of appetite, anemia, and kidney problems. Carrots, liver, milk, butter, cheese, and spinach are all rich sources of vitamin A.

The B complex of vitamins is also important. One of these is B_{12}, which plays a critical role in creating DNA and red and white blood cells. Too little B_{12} can result in anemia, fatigue, constipation, and loss of appetite. B_{12} is found in eggs, milk, meat, and some fortified cereals. Another B vitamin is folic acid, which helps the body maintain red blood cells, cell growth, and protein levels. Fortified breakfast cereals, liver, asparagus, spinach, and legumes are all good sources of folic acid.

Vitamin C helps the body absorb iron. It boosts the immune system, which fights off infections and other health woes, and is important in maintaining and repairing tissue, bones, and teeth. Too little vitamin C can result in anemia, loose teeth, joint pain, and hair loss. One well-known example of vitamin C deficiency occurred during the eighteenth century, when many sailors on long ocean voyages contracted a debilitating disease called scurvy. Scurvy can cause bleeding gums, weakness, and even death. The sailors discovered that they could prevent scurvy by making sure they ate enough fresh citrus fruit, which is rich in vitamin C. Other natural sources of vitamin C include broccoli, spinach, tomatoes, and potatoes.

Next in the list of important vitamins is D. Too little vitamin D can lead to serious bone and muscle problems. This is because vitamin D helps the body absorb calcium, which is crucial to building and maintaining muscles, bones, teeth, and nerves. Sunlight and dairy foods, like yogurt and milk, are abundant sources of vitamin D. It is also found in some fish, including sardines and canned salmon; fortified bread and tofu; and green vegetables, such as collard greens and okra.

The body also needs vitamin K, which aids in blood clotting and thus is vital to the ability to heal. Too little vitamin K results in excessive bruising and bleeding. Vitamin K is found naturally in green leafy vegetables as well as in soybeans and other plant foods.

Fat Soluble vs. Water Soluble

All of these vitamins can be divided into two categories: fat-soluble vitamins (able to dissolve in fat) and water-soluble vitamins (able to dissolve in water). Fat-soluble vitamins are

A, D, E, and K. Water-soluble vitamins are B and C. The difference is important because the two types act differently in the body.

Fat-soluble vitamins are stored in the body fat and tend to remain there. Water-soluble vitamins are not completely retained; instead, a high percentage of the vitamin is simply excreted in the urine. It is estimated that the average human body absorbs only about 15 to 25 percent of water-soluble vitamins that are ingested. This has led to the often-heard joke that "Americans have the most expensive urine in the world" because they spend millions of dollars every year on vitamins that mostly just get flushed out of their bodies.

It is important that people follow dosage instructions for vitamins because certain types—mostly of the fat-soluble variety—can cause vitamin toxicity (poisoning) if a person takes too much. The body cannot get rid of the excess. For example, people should not take more vitamin A than the

While taking vitamins in moderation can be beneficial, taking more than the recommended dose should never be done without medical supervision.

recommended upper limit (which most nutritionists place at three thousand micrograms). Symptoms of a vitamin A overdose can be severe and include dry skin, headache, nausea, dizziness, blurred vision, and loss of appetite. Vitamin A, along with the other fat-soluble vitamins, D, K, and E, is of particular concern because it remains in the body, is stored in fat, and is excreted very slowly. Iron supplements are especially risky if taken in very high doses. In fact, high doses are so toxic that they can be fatal.

In some cases, larger doses of vitamins and supplements are recommended by doctors. For example, extra iron is extremely important if a person is anemic and his/her body is not producing enough red blood cells. As with any major change in dietary habits, large doses of vitamins should be taken only with medical supervision. Some nutritionists advise dividing a large dose into smaller doses to be taken over the course of a day. That way, the body will have a chance to absorb as much as possible before it is excreted.

Finding and taking the right kinds and amounts of vitamins, minerals, and other nutrients is a complex process. All of these nutrients are crucial pieces of the good-nutrition puzzle. Making careful food choices, being aware of hidden food risk factors—such as trans fats—and selecting a safe, balanced vitamin regimen can help solve this puzzle and lead to a lifetime of better overall health.

CHAPTER 2

Nutrition and Metabolism

The word *metabolism* comes from a Greek word that means to change or to transform. Metabolism is a measure of how the body converts food and other substances into fuel. It is also a measure of how efficiently the body uses the energy that the fuel provides. Metabolism is a necessary process that allows the body to use food and other substances to maintain its regular functions, repair itself from damage and injury, and rid itself of toxins. In other words, metabolism is a necessary process, without which living organisms would die. It is also a fundamental part of the food/health equation. Yet the way metabolism works is complicated, and many mistaken (or unproven) ideas exist about it.

Metabolism is measured in calories. The metabolic rate is the amount of energy that the body uses in a day to perform the necessary actions to keep healthy and active. The amount of energy that comes from a diet of two thousand to twenty-eight hundred calories a day is considered a rough guideline for adequate metabolism. This, however, can vary greatly, depending on factors such as genetics and activity levels. In terms of health, maintaining a high level of metabolism through exercise and diet is considered good.

The body uses a great deal of energy during exercise, but it also uses energy even during inactivity. Lisa Balbach, a certified aerobics instructor and personal trainer, explains, "Whether you are eating, drinking, sleeping, cleaning etc. . . . your body is constantly burning calories to keep you going."[2] The rate at which people use energy when at rest is called the basal or resting metabolic rate. The resting metabolic rate, which is measured in calories, is the amount of energy the body uses while at rest to

The body uses a large amount of energy while exercising, but it also burns energy when you are sleeping, eating, or just hanging around doing nothing.

maintain basic functions like breathing and heart pumping. This number of calories and the energy used as the body moves around during the day (through exercise or walking) form a person's total energy needs.

Is Metabolism Inherited?

Metabolic traits can be inherited to a certain extent. For example, some people inherit a speedy metabolism, meaning their bodies burn calories at a faster rate than others, making it easier for them to lose weight or stay at a healthy weight. Other people have a slower metabolism, which may make it difficult for them to lose weight or prevent weight gain. In fact, a person's metabolism is directly linked to weight gain or loss. Robert Yanagisawa, director of the Medically Supervised Weight Management Program at Mount Sinai Medical Center in New York, comments, "The process of metabolism establishes the rate at which we burn our calories and, ultimately, how quickly we gain weight or how easily we lose it."[3]

Although factors such as genetics cannot be changed, it is still possible to improve the body's metabolic rate. This can be accomplished through a combination of exercise and diet. What kinds of food make up that diet—low versus high fat, for instance, or complex carbohydrates versus simple carbohydrates—also directly affect metabolism. Adding healthy sources of protein, such as fish, lean beef and pork, and white meat chicken, may be a good choice for improving a person's metabolic rate. According to the WebMD website, "The body burns up to twice as many calories digesting protein as it uses for fat or carbohydrates. Although you want to eat a balanced diet, replacing some carbs with lean, protein-rich foods can jump-start the metabolism at mealtime."[4]

Dietary factors can help determine how many calories are consumed and how quickly. In addition, water can have an effect on a person's metabolism, because the body needs water in order to process calories. In a person who is dehydrated—even only slightly—the metabolism may slow down. One study showed that adults who drank eight glasses or more of water each day burned more calories than adults who drank only four. Clearly, when it comes to metabolism, many factors are at play in addition to genetics.

Boosting Metabolism

People with more muscles burn calories faster. The WebMD website explains:

> Our bodies constantly burn calories, even when we're doing nothing. This resting metabolic rate is much higher in people with more muscle. Every pound of muscle uses about 6 calories a day just to sustain itself, while each pound of fat burns only 2 calories daily. That small difference can add up over time. In addition, after a bout of resistance training, muscles are activated all over your body, increasing your average daily metabolic rate.

WebMD, "Slideshow: 10 Ways to Boost Your Metabolism." http://women.webmd.com/family-health-9/slideshow-boost-your-metabolism.

Building muscle is an effective way to boost a person's metabolism and burn calories.

Male vs. Female Metabolism

Although heredity does play a part in determining metabolism, genetics alone does not govern a person's metabolism. How fast a person burns calories depends on several factors. One factor is gender and another factor is age.

Typically, men have a higher metabolism rate than women. This phenomenon is related to how the different genders store fat and how much is stored at a given time. Generally speaking, women tend to have a higher percentage of body fat than men. Good general measures for healthy ranges of body fat are 20 to 25 percent for women but only 10 to 15 percent for men.

While this man and woman are jogging at the same speed, the man's metabolic rate is higher than the woman's and is directly related to how differently the genders store fat.

The exact reasons for the difference in metabolism between men and women are still being studied. Evidence suggests that the answer lies partially in where the two sexes store fat. Typically, females store much of their fat in their hips and thighs, creating the so-called pear shape, while males store more in their abdominal (belly) region, giving rise to the so-called apple shape. Some studies indicate that abdominal fat is easier for the body to metabolize than fat in the hips and thighs.

Gender alone, however, does not generally have a significant effect on metabolic rates. Age also plays a role. Studies clearly show that both men and women, even with regular exercise, tend to gain weight as they age. This is because the body's metabolism begins to slow down about 5 percent each decade after age forty.

> # NUTRITION FACT
>
> ## 1 per year
> The number of pounds lost by drinking five to six glasses of water with ice per day

Extra Weight and Metabolism

If a person is overweight, more calories are burned at rest than if he or she were trimmer. This is because an overweight person's body has to work harder at rest to maintain basic functions like breathing and heart rate. Therefore, the metabolisms of overweight people may actually be faster, not slower. Yet this does not mean that someone who is overweight will burn enough calories just sitting around. The body burns far more calories while exercising than it does while resting.

In addition to weight, the amount of food consumed at each snack or meal also plays a part in metabolism. A number of studies show that people think they eat less than they actually do—and are surprised when they find out how many calories they actually consume. Several factors play a role in this illusion. For one thing, restaurants typically serve far more food in a portion than is needed, and people may overeat without realizing it. Eating with others, which typically happens in restaurants, also increases the chances of eating too much, perhaps because people get caught up in conversation. Eating alone at home can also be a major problem in controlling metabolism and weight. People who eat alone often read or watch television while doing so, and typically they do not pay close attention to how much they eat. It is easy to unknowingly overeat in such situations.

The Importance of Breakfast

Another important issue in metabolic rate is skipping meals. Many people believe that skipping a meal is a good idea for losing weight, but this is not true. In fact, skipping meals may actually cause weight gain. Studies indicate that people who skip at least one meal on a regular basis tend to be heavier than those who eat a regularly spaced set of meals, ideally a healthy breakfast plus three to five smaller meals throughout the rest of the day. This is because skipping a meal causes the body to act as if it is in starvation mode. The body then slows down its metabolism, compensating by conserving energy.

It is especially important to eat breakfast every day, because the body has already gone without eating for eight to ten hours or more. Skipping breakfast not only slows down the metabolism, it also leads to feeling very hungry by midmorning, and the temptation to eat will be strong. In addition, skipping breakfast can make a person feel tired and empty during the day. Columbia University's Health Services likens the process of having some food in the stomach to driving a car. It states, "If you hit the road without any breakfast, you'll be running on fumes, not fuel. It's like choosing not to put gas into your car before driving to work. A few gallons will get you farther than if your tank is on or below empty."[5]

Just as crucial as actually eating breakfast is making the right choice about what to eat for breakfast. Eating a good breakfast will help control hunger later in the day, but not all typical breakfast foods are created equal. Many common breakfast foods, such as pastries, bagels, and toast and jam, are mostly simple carbohydrates. This type of carbohydrate will be satisfying for a little while, but in about half an hour the body will need something more. The problem can be solved by eating something other than simple carbohydrates instead. Anything that has a little

Eating a healthy breakfast in the morning is essential in order to rev up the body's metabolism after a night's sleep.

protein, a little fat, and some complex carbohydrates is a better option. Whole-grain cereal with low-fat or fat-free milk, an egg and toast, or a low-fat fruit smoothie are all good breakfast choices.

Cereals, whether hot or cold, can also be excellent choices for breakfast. Yet different cereals have different nutritional values. The body tends to digest some low-fiber cereals, such as Cream of Wheat, very quickly; as a result, these cereals will not create a very full feeling. The satisfaction of a low-fiber cereal will not last long. High-fiber cereals, however, like cooked oatmeal, are digested slowly. These cereals help keep the metabolism steady and make a person feel fuller, less tempted to overeat, and less likely to get hungry again soon.

Eating Small, Frequent Meals

Some people seem to eat whatever they want, and they do not gain weight. The chances are good that these people simply eat smaller portions on a regular basis. For the same reason that eating breakfast helps boost a person's metabolism, eating healthy, nutritious snacks throughout the day also helps keep the metabolism steady and can be a benefit when trying to lose weight, since going too long between meals can result in overeating at a later meal.

In a 2005 study conducted at Georgia State University, researchers found that when athletes ate three snacks of about 250 calories each per day, they had more energy than when they did not snack. In addition, snacking helped the athletes eat less at each of their three mealtimes. By snacking, these athletes took in fewer calories overall, reduced their body fat, and increased their metabolic rate.

In fact, eating small but frequent meals is generally good for overall health, assuming that daily food choices and amounts are healthy and nutritious. The calories consumed in small, frequent meals are used only as needed. The WebMD website explains:

> Eating more really can help you lose weight—eating more often, that is. When you eat large meals with many hours in between, you train your metabolism to slow down. Having a small meal or snack every 3 to 4 hours keeps your metabolism cranking, so you burn more calories over the course of a day. Several studies have also shown that people who snack regularly eat less at meal time.[6]

Many nutritionists recommend a meal pattern of three small meals and two to three small snacks. This not only helps boost the metabolism, but it also helps a person avoid getting fatigued during the day. An ideal regimen might be breakfast at 7:00 A.M., lunch at 11:00 A.M., a snack at 3:00 P.M., dinner at 6:00 P.M., and a bedtime snack at 9:00

Many nutritionists recommend three small meals and two to three snacks a day to keep the body's metabolism running efficiently.

or 10:00 P.M. If a person's day is longer or shorter than this time frame, the person just needs to remember to eat at least something every three to four hours. In addition, whereas breakfast should be the biggest meal of the day in order to jump-start the body's metabolism, dinner should be the lightest meal. Some experts recommend not eating anything any later than three to four hours before bedtime. This will help the body burn off calories while the person is awake and more active.

Eating something healthy and nutritious every few hours also helps ensure that the body's blood sugar levels remain more stable. Stable blood sugar levels in turn helps provide a steady source of energy to keep a person's metabolism steady. HealthyNewAge.com explains the importance of maintaining a balanced metabolism: "An imbalanced or sluggish metabolism can cause many poor health effects and symptoms such as weight gain, indigestion, lethargy, fatigue and poor immune response."[7] In addition to keeping the metabolism balanced, stable blood sugar levels also help keep the brain alert. In fact, overeating is a big reason that people often feel sluggish after consuming a large meal.

If a person has a generally healthy diet and stable metabolism, having an occasional order of fries is not a big deal. The occasional indulgence is not nearly as important as watching what is eaten most of the time. The truth is simple: The body gains weight when it takes in more calories than it needs. But taking in those calories slowly and regularly, rather than in huge and less-frequent meals, is best for keeping metabolism steady.

Supplements and Metabolism

The importance of not skipping meals, eating healthy foods for meals and snacks, and eating small, frequent meals and snacks is well established. Any benefits the body may gain from supplements, however, is not as certain. Broadly speaking, a nutritional supplement is any substance that is ingested—usually in pill form—in addition to food in order to boost the nutritional content in the body. For example,

Does Eating Turkey Make You Sleepy?

A long-held belief is that eating turkey makes people sleepy. But people who find themselves needing a nap on Thanksgiving should not blame the turkey. Turkey contains L-tryptophan, an amino acid that has been associated with a calming effect and better sleep. In order for L-tryptophan to work that way, however, it has to be eaten on an empty stomach and without any other amino acids or proteins. Because turkey contains plenty of protein (and it is certainly not the only food on the Thanksgiving table), the meat will not have enough L-tryptophan to make a difference.

The real reason people get sleepy after a Thanksgiving feast is due to a combination of factors having nothing to do with what is in the food: holiday stress, the hours spent in the kitchen cooking, and, in particular, the huge amount of food consumed. Eating a massive amount of food causes the body to send a lot of its blood supply to the stomach to help with digestion, so there is less flowing to the brain. The result is sluggishness and a strong desire to nap.

WebMD, "Slideshow: 10 Ways to Boost Your Metabolism." http://women.webmd.com/family-health-9/slideshow-boost-your-metabolism.

Though turkey contains the sleep-inducing amino acid L-Tryptophan, other proteins and amino acids in the meal cause the sleepy feeling one gets after the Thanksgiving meal.

vitamins, minerals, herbs, and sports nutrition products, such as drinks or bars that contain electrolytes, are all food supplements. Natural herbal supplements have become very popular in the last four or five decades to cure or ward off a variety of maladies, although it has not been proven that herbal supplements are necessarily effective in preventing or treating disease.

Many supplements are advertised as being good for raising metabolism, and this assertion is widely believed. Some people swear by capsules containing ginseng or red pepper; others insist that green tea—consumed either as a beverage or as a capsule containing green tea extract—does the trick. No proof exists, however, that any of these supplements are effective.

Some claims about the benefits of supplements are probably based on the fact that calories from any source will temporarily rev up the metabolism. Molly Kimball, a registered dietician and a sports and lifestyle nutritionist at the Ochsner Hospital's Elmwood Fitness Center in New Orleans, Louisiana, explains, "Actually, any food will increase your metabolism, mostly in the first hour after you eat—that's when your system is most revved."[8] Yet no study has proven that any single food increases metabolism for more than about an hour. This is because the body adapts to whatever substances a person ingests, so any temporary "boost" a food or supplement provides will level out over time.

> ## NUTRITION FACT
>
> ### 2 per day
> The amount of calories burned by each pound of fat

It is wise to be skeptical when a supplement is guaranteed to produce certain results, such as boosting the metabolism. Statistics and studies are often misstated or flat out wrong in advertisements. In addition, anecdotal information or unreliable sources can be wildly inaccurate. Consumers should be sure their information comes from reputable sources. The website of the U.S. Food and Drug Administration offers this advice: "Learn to distinguish hype from evidence-based science. Nonsensical lingo can sound very convincing."[9]

Getting good, reliable information is a vital step in keeping the metabolism operating at its most efficient level. Maintaining an optimum metabolism plays an important role in overall nutrition. A balanced metabolism contributes significantly to the body's ability to absorb and use caloric energy and to perform other crucial jobs. Furthermore, a person's activity level also affects how calories are used. Regular exercise reduces body fat, increases lean muscle mass, and burns calories more efficiently—all things that can help boost metabolism.

CHAPTER 3

Nutrition and Exercise

The benefits of good nutrition cannot be considered without also examining exercise, because nutrition and exercise are deeply intertwined. Working together, both are key ingredients for weight control, increased stamina, resistance to disease, and other aspects of good health.

Aerobic Exercise

Exercise is critical for optimum health. Most basic health guidelines recommend regular exercise routines for people without disabilities or other health issues. The two kinds of physical activity recommended are aerobic and muscle-strengthening exercises.

Aerobic exercise increases oxygen intake and requires the heart and lungs to work hard to deliver extra oxygen to the arms and legs. It is typically measured as light, moderate, and vigorous. Examples of light exercise are doing laundry, cooking, or shopping. For an average healthy person, this is too little to be of significant value.

Moderate exercise might take the form of walking, bicycling, or swimming. While engaged in moderate exercise, people generally break into a sweat and raise their heart rate. One rule of thumb for judging moderate exercise is that people should still be able to comfortably carry on a conversation or sing a song while exercising. This would not be possible during vigorous aerobic exercise. Examples of vigorous exercise include jogging or playing a fast game of basketball.

The Centers for Disease Control and Prevention (CDC) recommends a minimum of 150 minutes a week of moderate to vigorous aerobic exercise. The agency's guidelines suggest that this activity be spread out over a week, for at least ten minutes at a time. The CDC also provides this guideline: One minute of vigorous-intensity activity roughly equals two minutes of moderate-intensity activity.

An aerobic workout can be accomplished by swimming or bicycling, among other activities.

Jane E. Brody, a nutrition and personal health columnist for the *New York Times*, writes, "The single most effective activity, studies have found, is an aerobic activity like brisk walking—about 30 minutes a day. If you can't get out of the house, walk inside. Go up and down stairs, walk the hall, walk from room to room, walk in place. If walking doesn't suit you, try dancing to music."[10]

Strengthening Muscles

In addition to aerobic activity, experts recommend doing muscle-strengthening exercises at least twice weekly. These activities should work all the major muscle groups of the body: legs, hips, back, chest, abdomen, shoulders, and arms. Examples of muscle-strengthening activities are weight lifting, yoga, and exercises such as push-ups and sit-ups. Although muscle-strengthening exercises can be done on the same days as aerobic activities, they do not count toward the aerobic exercise total.

When starting an exercise regimen, experts recommend building slowly from moderate to vigorous activity rather than trying to do too much too quickly. It is also a good idea to find ways to keep exercise interesting, such as exercising with friends or listening to music while working out.

Experts also stress the importance of finding a comfortable routine and sticking with it. The American College of Sports Medicine notes, "Starting an exercise program can sound like a daunting task, but just remember that your main goal is to meet the basic physical activity recommendations."[11]

Staying Hydrated

Getting enough liquids is essential for optimal health, particularly when exercising. Many people who regularly exercise mistakenly believe that sports drinks or water should only be consumed after a workout. In fact, the benefits of hydration are most effective when liquid is consumed before, during, and after exercising. Anyone doing exercise should begin a workout already fully hydrated. This is especially important for serious athletes, according to the American

The human body should get 2 to 4 pints (0.9L to 1.9L) of liquid a day to replace loss, depending on the level of physical exertion.

College of Sports Medicine. This organization recommends that athletes drink 16 ounces (0.47L) of fluids a couple of hours before starting sports practice, plus more during and after the workout as well.

Water is the most important liquid in terms of staying hydrated. It is also the body's single most important nutrient. The human body can typically survive for several weeks without food, but it will last only a few days without water.

Thus, the issue of drinking sufficient water is crucial to health. The body needs to stay hydrated, and a common recommendation is to drink eight glasses of liquid a day. The liquid, however, does not have to be just water.

On average, if a person is fairly sedentary, he or she loses daily about 2 pints (0.9L) of liquid from breathing, sweating, and excreting urine. Many experts therefore recommend a minimum of 2 pints (0.9L) of liquid a day to replenish this loss. Some nutritionists advise 4 pints (1.9L) or more a day, even for people who live in a cool climate. This amount increases with exercise.

Still, people do not need to guzzle water all day. This is because the liquid the body consumes does not need to all come from drinking. Foods, especially fruits, vegetables, and soups, can provide a large proportion of a person's water intake. Recent research indicates that liquid from these sources keeps the body hydrated just as well as water does. So 4 pints (1.9L) of liquid a day, counting drinking water and liquid from other sources, may be enough, unless the weather has been especially hot or if a person has been ill or exercising heavily—in which case, more is probably needed.

Even soda can be helpful for keeping the body hydrated, but the key is to drink it in moderation. Aside from the extra empty calories, lots of soda will mean an excess of phosphoric acid, which interferes with the body's ability to use calcium properly. Studies indicate that people who frequently consume soft drinks can suffer from weakened bone structures.

NUTRITION FACT

57 gallons

The amount of soft drinks consumed per person in the United States in 2002

Bottled vs. Tap Water

The United States has some of the cleanest tap water in the world, and it is available to the majority of the nation's households. Government agencies regulate it to a degree, in an effort to make sure that it remains safe. Agency actions are based largely on the Safe Drinking Water Act, the federal law governing the nation's water supply.

Changing Habits

People use many excuses to resist making healthy changes. They often complain that such changes are too expensive, too time-consuming, too hard to do, or too boring. The Weight-control Information Network website, a service of the National Institute of Diabetes and Digestive and Kidney Diseases of the National Institutes of Health, points out that change is not easy, but it is possible. It states,

> Change is always possible, and a person is never too out-of-shape, overweight, or old to make healthy changes. . . .
>
> Old habits die hard. If you want to change your habits, you may find it helpful to make realistic and gradual changes one step at a time and at your own pace. It is important to think about what motivates you, what trips you up, and what you enjoy when it comes to eating and activity habits. There is no such thing as a "one-size-fits-all" approach.

Weight-control Information Network, "Changing Your Habits: Steps to Better Health." http://win.niddk.nih.gov/publications/changing-habits.htm.

Some critics, however, argue that America's drinking water is not regulated enough. According to a 2009 article in the *New York Times*, the regulations for drinking water are badly outdated. These regulations concern hundreds of chemicals used in industry and agriculture that can find their way into water supplies. The *Times* reviewed some 19 million test results from the District of Columbia and forty-five states. It concluded that "more than 62 million Americans have been exposed since 2004 to drinking water that did not meet at least one commonly used government health guideline intended to help protect people from cancer or serious disease."[12]

Supporters of the existing regulations argue that the fact that drinking water may not meet federal health guidelines is not necessarily dangerous because the chemicals are in very small doses. They argue that these chemicals would have to be consumed over many years to have any effect. These supporters also say that the cost of removing tiny amounts of chemicals would be prohibitively expensive. Furthermore, these supporters point out, it would be impossible to effectively regulate the nation's nearly sixty thousand water districts.

In the wake of concerns about tap water, the popularity of bottled water has skyrocketed. The bottled water industry has become a multibillion-dollar business, with huge advertising budgets spent to convince the public that one kind of water is better than another. Yet despite lavish claims about the purity of mountain springs and other enticements, it has not been clearly shown that bottled water is significantly healthier than average tap water. In fact, studies indicate that a significant proportion of bottled water simply comes from city water supplies. (Often this water is filtered and minerals are added before bottling.) Critics further contend that the bottled water industry is as severely underregulated as the nation's tap water supply.

The trend toward bottled water has also come under scrutiny for its role in the overall degradation of the environment. Estimates vary widely, but as many as 50 billion plastic water bottles may be used every year in the United States alone. These bottles are recyclable, but it is estimated that only about one-third of them actually reach recycling centers.

Sports Drinks

Sports drinks have become widely used by athletes in recent years in the hopes that they provide some advantage over plain water. Are sports drinks really better than plain water when exercising? Generally speaking, the answer is yes. When exercising, it is especially important to drink plenty of liquid. Exercise quickly dehydrates the body through

Fully Caffeinated

Energy drinks have become popular in recent years. One problem, however, is that their energy boost is fueled by high levels of caffeine. Below is the caffeine content in some popular energy drinks.

Sports or Energy Drink	Serving Size	Caffeine (milligrams)
AMP	8.4 ounces (250mL)	74 mg
Enviga	12 ounces (355mL)	100 mg
Full Throttle	16 ounces (480mL)	144 mg
Monster Energy	16 ounces (480mL)	160 mg
No Fear	8 ounces (240mL)	83 mg
No Name (formerly known as Cocaine)	8.4 ounces (250mL)	280 mg
Red Bull	8.3 ounces (250mL)	76 mg
Rockstar	8 ounces (240mL)	80 mg

To put this in perspective, a single shot of Starbucks espresso has between 58 and 75 milligrams of caffeine, a Starbucks Tazo chai tea has 100 milligrams, but Coke (zero, classic, regular, or diet) has only 35 milligrams of caffeine.

Taken from: MayoClinic.com, "Nutrition and Healthy Eating," www.mayoclinic.com/health/caffeine/AN01211.

sweat, and dehydration can lead to muscle cramps, quickened heartbeats, a light-headed feeling, and fatigue.

In the case of moderate exercise, water is usually sufficient. Yet sports drinks are better choices when working hard and sweating hard, such as during a strenuous exercise routine, running, or playing an intense sport. This is because sports drinks replenish the body's electrolytes—minerals (including calcium, phosphorous, and magnesium) that carry an electrical charge through the body's blood and other fluids. Electrolytes have several important functions, including helping to maintain electrical contact across cell membranes and transmitting electrical impulses that control muscle contractions and blood acidity.

Some energy drinks contain high levels of caffeine, which can cause nervousness, irritability, and increased blood pressure.

Many sports drinks are available on the market, but their formulas vary a great deal. Some are better for exercise and overall health than others. For example, some have about half the calories and sugar of fruit juice or soft drinks, while others have more. Unless high-intensity exercise regularly burns off the extra calories, there will be an increased risk of weight gain.

There are also various waters available on the market that are supplemented with vitamins. Studies indicate that they have no significant nutritional value, although they are still valuable for overall hydration. The healthy ingredients that some of these waters claim to include may not actually be present. In 2009 the Center for Science in the Public Interest sued the maker of one line of vitamin waters for what it called deceptive and unsubstantiated claims. (As of mid-2010 the suit is still pending.) Many experts maintain that vitamin waters are being marketed simply as a way for the bottled water industry to boost profits. Marion Nestle, a professor of nutrition studies at New York University, comments, "Vitamins, color, herbs, protein, and all the other additions to water—those are a marketing ploy."[13]

Some of the ingredients—notably caffeine—found in certain sports drinks (and energy drinks as well) can have negative side effects, particularly for people with heart conditions. Even if a person does not have heart problems, the caffeine in many sports drinks can cause nervousness, irritability, an increase in blood pressure, and an increased heartbeat. Caffeine can also cause sleep loss, which can certainly affect mental and physical performance.

Many factors must be considered when assessing the health benefits or drawbacks of water, sports drinks, and other beverages. As with food in general, it is important to pay attention to nutrition labels and other sources of information when choosing or rejecting a drink. No matter what, it remains vitally important to make sure that enough liquid—from a variety of sources—is part of a regular, healthy diet.

Eating and Exercise

When it comes to eating and exercise, a number of mistaken ideas exist. For example, some people think it is helpful to have a piece of candy before exercising to give them an energy boost. The truth is that simple sugars, such as those found in candy bars, do quickly provide a short burst of energy. Eating candy or another source of simple sugar before exercising is not a good idea, however. Simple sugars cannot provide long-term energy for stamina, and they have precious few other nutrients.

Another commonly held myth is that exercisers need plenty of sodium to replace the salt they lose through sweating. This is true only if the exercise is very strenuous. A moderate amount of perspiration will not typically have a big impact on the body's sodium level. It is more important to replace the overall liquid level with water or a sports drink. Some sports drinks contain sodium, but they often have too little to make a difference, so they should not be relied on to replenish sodium.

> **NUTRITION FACT**
>
> **35 percent**
> National average percentage of adults meeting the CDC's recommended amount of physical activity (150 minutes weekly) in 2007

Occasional Treats

Eating a nutritious diet does not mean giving up favorite foods, even if the favorite foods are not the healthiest choices. The trick is to avoid eating only the unhealthy favorite foods. A diet that is generally healthy can tolerate an occasional treat, such as a slice of pizza, an ice cream sundae, or some french fries. Nutritionist Katherine Zeratsky, using diet soda as an example, comments:

> Drinking a reasonable amount of diet soda a day, such as a can or two, isn't likely to hurt you. . . . But diet soda isn't a health drink or a silver bullet for weight loss. . . .

> Healthier choices abound. Start your day with a small glass of 100 percent fruit juice. Drink skim milk with meals. Sip water throughout the day. For variety, try sparkling water or add a squirt of lemon or cranberry juice to your water. Save diet soda for an occasional treat.

Katherine Zeratsky. "Diet Soda: Is It Bad for You?" MayoClinic.com. www.mayo clinic.com/health/diet-soda/AN01732.

While an occasional can of diet soda is okay, a healthier choice for everyday consumption is 100 percent fruit juice or other healthy beverage.

On the other hand, people definitely should boost their salt intake if they are doing something really strenuous, such as running a marathon or doing heavy labor in hot weather. Salt helps the body regulate its fluid balance, and it is also needed for nerves and muscles to work properly. Extra sodium, perhaps taken as salt tablets, plus sports drinks can help in this case. Sports drinks are advised because the potassium they contain helps digest the extra salt. Too much salt, however, can result in high blood pressure and other problems, so salt intake should always be carefully controlled.

Another common misconception is that it is better to exercise with an empty stomach because this will cause the body to burn off excess fat. What really happens, however, is that if the brain senses an empty stomach, it perceives that the body is starving. It then automatically goes into survival mode and tells the body to do everything it can to retain the fat that it already has. Instead of using this body fat for immediate fuel, which would be a good thing, it uses some of its muscle tissue, which is not good.

Many nutritionists recommend that 50 to 55 percent of the body's energy intake should come from carbohydrates; for athletes it should be increased to 60 to 70 percent.

The types of food people eat are important when it comes to exercise, because these foods directly affect the success of working out or playing a sport. For example, getting sufficient complex carbohydrates, such as those found in fruit and starches, is essential to exercise. Complex carbohydrates are digested slowly, so they provide long-term stores of energy. Many sources recommend that 50 to 55 percent of the body's energy intake should come from carbohydrates; for athletes, that should be boosted to 60 or even 70 percent.

Protein is another crucial diet element for optimum exercise or athletics. The best amount of protein depends on gender, weight, and other factors. The website SportsMed Web advises 3.2 ounces (91g) of protein daily for a 150-pound (68kg) male triathlete, and 2.8 ounces (79g) for a 115-pound (52kg) female high school track runner.

Eating the right foods at the right times and in the right amounts is a necessary and important component of a program for good general health—just as exercise is. Exercise and proper nutrition, in turn, are closely connected to a related and much-discussed issue: keeping a healthy weight.

CHAPTER 4

Maintaining a Healthy Weight

Many people have wanted to lose weight at some point in their lives. Television programs, such as *The Biggest Loser*; dieting books; and other weight-loss products form a multibillion-dollar industry. In the United States losing weight is a contentious issue. Partly out of vanity, and partly out of genuine interest in becoming healthier, millions of Americans try out one new diet after another, constantly searching for one that will keep the pounds off over the long-term.

Every year dozens of new diets trumpet new methods. They claim that following certain rules—measuring every single meal, for instance, or restricting what is eaten to just a few specific foods—will lead to permanent weight loss. The truth is that going on a diet to lose a few pounds—perhaps before bathing-suit season—will only be a temporary fix. Instead, it is smarter to find a suitable eating plan that will succeed over the long run. The basis of any plan to lose weight or maintain a healthy weight should still be that simple-but-difficult formula: Burn off more calories than are consumed.

If a plan like that can be successfully carried out, dropping pounds and keeping them off will be easier. Christopher Gardner, an assistant professor of nutritional science

Many new diet plans surface each year, but the basis for a healthy weight is to burn off more calories than you consume.

at the Stanford University School of Medicine, says, "A diet won't work if you think of it as doing a different thing for a while and then you're going to stop doing it. If you have a new way of eating and think, I'm going to eat like this forever, that's the way to lose weight."[14] Yet ideas about proper long-term diets vary widely. For example, some people swear that vegetarianism—avoiding meat (and, in some cases, fish as well)—is the way to go. Others insist that humans have always eaten meat and still need at least some of it in their diets.

It is important to realize that diets are not one-size-fits-all eating plans. No single diet will produce long-term weight loss for everyone. There are numerous fad diets around, but these generally do not take into account the simple fact that people's bodies are different. This fact creates dramatic differences in how individuals react to changes in their diet. What works for one person may not work for another.

Fat Free vs. Calorie Free

As part of modern society's widespread desire to lose weight, dozens of misconceptions exist. One is especially pervasive: The misconception that foods labeled as "fat free," "low fat," or "reduced fat" are necessarily low in calories, too.

These labels can mislead consumers. Food can be low fat, or even fat free, and still have plenty of calories. The National Heart, Lung, and Blood Institute explains, "A calorie is a calorie is a calorie whether it comes from fat or carbohydrate. Anything eaten in excess can lead to weight gain. . . . Just because a product is fat-free, it doesn't mean that it is 'calorie-free.'"[15] Many people mistakenly believe that because a food is low fat or fat free, they can eat more of it and not gain weight. However, with increased consumption also comes an increase in the number of calories taken in.

Compounding misconceptions about lower-fat food is the fact that when fat is removed from food, a lot of the flavor and texture is lost. Often, as with some brands of yogurt, extra sugars and other additives make up for this loss. In addition, the difference in calories is often insignificant when comparing fat-free foods with their higher-fat counterparts. For example, two fat-free fig cookies have only nine fewer calories than two regular fig cookies. A 0.5-cup (118ml) serving of nonfat vanilla frozen yogurt has only four fewer calories than the same amount of regular vanilla frozen yogurt. While one reduced-fat Oreo has about forty-seven calories, one regular Oreo cookie has about fifty-three calories.

These figures suggest that dieters need to monitor both the number of calories and the amount of fat in foods they eat. In fact, research cited by several organizations indicates that successful dieters are often those who maintain correct calorie intake while eating a diet that is higher in carbohydrates and lower in fat. But just as with lower-fat foods, there are a number of mistaken beliefs about carbohydrates, particularly when it comes to complex carbohydrates, or starches.

Starches

One common belief among dieters is that starchy food is fattening, but this is not necessarily true. Everyone needs a certain amount of starch for proper nutrition. Starchy foods are important because, as carbohydrates, they provide energy for muscles and the brain.

Furthermore, many starchy foods, like bread, rice, pasta, cereals, beans, and potatoes, are naturally low in both fat and calories. A medium-size potato has only about 110 calories, for instance, and a slice of whole-grain wheat bread has about 70. The problems come when high-fat toppings like butter, sour cream, or peanut butter and jelly are added to these low-calorie items.

At the same time, it is important to note the amount of starchy foods consumed. Pasta, for example, is nearly fat free and thus can be a good weight-loss food. But 1 cup (237ml) of pasta has 40 grams of carbohydrates, so even a small bowl can quickly push the body's carbohydrate intake too high. One solution to the problem is to eat less pasta while pairing it with fiber-rich, low-carbohydrate, low-calorie vegetables, like broccoli, green beans, cauliflower, and mushrooms. Roughly equal amounts of veggies and pasta will keep the body's carbohydrate and calorie content under control; provide vitamins, minerals, and fiber; and still make a satisfyingly full meal.

Fruit and Weight Loss

Like pasta and other starches, fruit, and fruit juice are all excellent additions to any healthy eating plan, especially for weight loss. Generally speaking, however, fresh fruit is better than juice for dieting. This is true for a couple of reasons. Many fruit juices contain added sugar beyond what is naturally found in fruit. This is especially likely if they are not labeled as being 100 percent fruit juice. And even if juices have only the sugars naturally found in fruit, they will provide calories without completely satisfying the appetite.

Another disadvantage to fruit juice is that it is easy to drink too much of it. Some nutritionists say that doing so on a regular basis—even a glass or two a day—can increase a daily calorie count beyond its optimum level. In contrast, fresh fruit provides several vitamins and fiber that juice cannot. The fiber is especially important for dieting. It will satisfy hunger more efficiently than juice, and thus decrease the chances of overeating. Therefore, fresh fruit is generally better for dieters. An exception to this general rule is freshly squeezed citrus juice, such as orange or grapefruit juice, because it contains pulp. The pulp is fiber, and it will better serve the purpose of satisfying hunger than clear juices. Whole fruit, however, still has much more fiber and is still the best choice.

When it comes to calories, however, all fruit is not equal. For example, dried fruit may not help with weight control. First, during the drying process, sugar is sometimes added to certain dried fruits, such as cranberries, because they are so tart. Second, a given amount of dried fruit typically has more calories than an equivalent amount of fresh fruit. This is because the dehydration process concentrates the natural sugars in the fruit, so less is typically needed to have the same number of calories. For example, 1.5 cups (355ml) of grapes has about 60 calories, but just 1 cup (237ml) of raisins, the dried equivalent of grapes, has a whopping 525 calories. This increase is not because the manufacturer has added sugar to the raisins. It is simply because raisins take up much less space than grapes.

> ## NUTRITION FACT
> ### Over 3,500
> Number of calories the body needs to burn in order to lose one pound a week

Salads

Vegetables are excellent for general health, and like fruit, they can be a big factor in weight loss. It is a common belief that eating a salad is an excellent way to diet because salads are always low in fat. Yet this is not necessarily the case. One problem is that added dressings and ingredients, such as ranch dressing or chunks of whole-milk cheese, can be very high in fat. Also, the ingredients in salads usually have few starchy carbohydrates, and a shortage of starchy carbohydrates will not satisfy hunger. The temptation to snack after the meal or later in the day then increases, and people

Salads can be a healthy food choice as long as fatty salad dressings and other high calorie toppings, such as cheese or croutons, are avoided.

may choose fattening snacks like cookies or ice cream. Eating a salad can thus be a good idea for dieting—but only if it is not packed with extra calories, and it contains (or, more likely, is accompanied by) sufficient complex carbohydrates.

Eating salads as a way to diet is especially tricky when it comes to the salads commonly served at fast-food restaurants. It is not always true that the foods purported to be healthy at fast-food restaurants, including salads, really are less fattening than burgers. Some salads and dressings at these restaurants can be very high in fat (and salt as well). For example, a house salad with grilled chicken and Thousand Island dressing from Zaxby's has 871 calories and sixty-eight grams of fat. Compare that to a McDonald's Big Mac, which has 590 calories and thirty-four grams of fat.

Vegetarian Diets and Meat Consumption

Every year people all around the world choose to forgo meat in favor of greens in order to manage their weight and improve their health. Several well-respected studies show that avoiding or restricting meats can contribute to good health, since so many kinds of meat are high in fat. Research also shows that people who choose to eat a vegetarian diet, also known as vegetarians, consume fewer calories and generally have lower body weight/height ratios than nonvegetarians. The problem is that some vegetarians do not take care to maintain a balanced diet.

A successful vegetarian diet requires eating a wide and carefully selected range of foods, with an emphasis on vegetables, fruits, complex carbohydrates, protein, and healthy fats. If people choose to avoid meat, they must be doubly sure to get enough nutrients elsewhere. Nutrients commonly lacking from vegetarian diets include iron, zinc, vitamin B_{12}, calcium, and protein.

Some people, known as vegans, choose not to eat meat, fish, dairy, and eggs. With a diet like this, vegans need to give even more thought and consideration to ensuring that they are getting sufficient nutrients. Choosing to skip meat has a number of benefits beyond just weight loss. Some people have moral objections to eating animals. Some simply feel better if they eat vegetarian. For many a primary reason for adopting vegetarianism is weight loss. A vegetarian diet can indeed be useful for this. Still, if all a person wants to do is lose weight, vegetarianism can be a bad choice without proper thought.

For one thing, "vegetarian" does not necessarily equal "low fat." Getting calories from full-fat foods such as cheese, nuts, and milk, which are popular with many vegetarians, can really add up. Likewise, it is important to consider cooking methods. For example, deep-fried french fries are meatless, but that does not make them healthy. From a weight-loss

> # NUTRITION FACT
> ## 1 pound
> Average amount of weight people gain eating over the year-end holiday season

standpoint, it does not make sense to stop eating meat and then simply replace it with other foods that are just as fattening—or even more fattening.

Commonly eaten meats, such as beef, chicken, and pork, can be unhealthy in other ways as well. Large amounts of these foods provide more protein than is necessary. For this reason, many nutritionists feel that the average American eats far too much meat.

On the other hand, meat is not necessarily evil from a health standpoint. For one thing, it is an excellent source of nutrients. Three small servings a week of lean red meat will provide the right balance of iron, zinc, vitamin B_{12}, and protein. The key word here is *small*. Another key word is *lean*. It is also important to avoid processed meats like salami, many of which have substances that have been linked with certain cancers.

Raw Vegetables

Some vegetarians—and even nonvegetarians—are embracing raw vegetables as a dietary choice. The concept of eating raw vegetables in place of cooked vegetables is not new. Since the mid-1980s, however, it has become increasingly popular.

Some vegetables are fine when eaten raw, and some vegetables, especially those high in fiber, are better when slightly cooked. Gentle cooking methods for vegetables, such as steaming, baking, broiling, microwaving, and stir-frying with a minimum of fat, can result in a healthier meal than eating their raw equivalents. This is because starches are harder to digest when they are raw, so the body digests some vegetables more easily when they are cooked; this, in turn, causes more nutrients to be absorbed. In general, though, people should avoid overcooked veggies. Too much heat can destroy the nutritive value of vegetables and spoil their flavor.

Organic Foods

Organic foods are those that have been produced without antibiotics, hormones, pesticides, irradiation, or bioengineering. The U.S. Department of Agriculture and the U.S.

Nutrients for Vegetarians

Vegetarians need to be especially careful about getting enough protein and other nutrients. Here are some good nonmeat sources:

Protein: eggs, beans, peas, nuts, seeds, tofu, and soy burgers

- Iron: cashews, spinach, lentils, garbanzo beans, and fortified bread or cereal

- Calcium: dairy, fortified soy-based products, collard greens, kale, and broccoli

- Vitamin D: fortified products, including milk, soy, and cereal

- Vitamin B_{12}: eggs, dairy, fortified cereal or soy beverages, tempeh, and miso

- Zinc: whole grains, nuts, tofu, and leafy vegetables such as spinach, cabbage, and lettuce

Adapted from the Weight-control Information Network's "Weight Loss and Nutrition Myths," March 2009. http://win.niddk.nih.gov/publications/myths.htm.

Food and Drug Administration certify that foods are organic. An ongoing debate, however, is whether organic produce is healthier than nonorganic produce.

People often choose organic food because they think it is safer, and many people believe organic food simply tastes better. Significant evidence supports the idea that eating mostly organically grown food is a healthy idea. Some critics, however, point out drawbacks.

Organic food is generally more expensive because producing it is more labor intensive. More importantly, under current regulations, food labeled as organic is not necessarily higher in nutritional quality. Studies into the nutritional content of organic versus nonorganic foods have shown some organic produce to contain slightly higher amounts of trace minerals, vitamin C, and antioxidants. However, these studies have been few and the findings have been mixed. According to the Mayo Clinic, a leading source of health and nutrition information, "No conclusive evidence shows that organic food is more nutritious than is conventionally grown food. Most experts agree that the amount of pesticides found on fruits and vegetables poses a very small health risk."[16]

Popular Fad Diets

Many factors are involved in finding the right eating plan for losing weight. It is difficult, and millions of people struggle every year to find a plan that will work for them. In the search for such a plan, alternative and fad diets are always

One of the more famous diets is the Atkins diet, which greatly limits carbohydrates, such as breads and fruits, and allows the consumption of high-fat-content foods such as red meats and cheese. Some nutritionists have questioned the diet's validity.

Dubious Diets

Strange theories about nutrition have been around for a long time. In the 1800s Sylvester Graham, an American dietitian and inventor of the graham cracker, had many ideas. Many were sound (for example, that chemical additives in bread are unhealthy), but some were not. According to Graham, people should never eat hot food, never drink water while eating, and avoid tea because it causes hallucinations.

In the late 1960s and early 1970s, there was the Sleeping Beauty diet, in which people were drugged to stay asleep for several days in hopes of waking up thinner. Likewise, the Calories Don't Count diet was equally dubious. According to that plan, a person could eat as much high-protein food as desired as long as he or she took a concentrated vegetable-oil pill supplied by the diet's inventor.

popular. Fad diets have many faithful followers—but are these diets any good? One expert who says no is Andrew Hill, a professor of medical psychology at Leeds University in England. He explains,

> People are looking for quick-fix repairs, but in fact they are very rare, particularly in relation to being overweight. The idea that some new discovery or new way of combining food will give you an instant fix to your weight or health problem is nearly always misinformed. Health isn't immediately reparable; weight isn't immediately modifiable.[17]

Typical of the fad-diet phenomenon is the Atkins diet. This plan calls for a regimen of eating that is low in carbohydrates but very high in fat. Its benefits have been questioned by many nutritionists, however, because a higher fat intake is closely linked to an increased risk of heart disease, diabetes, and other issues.

Another well-known fad diet is Sugar Busters! This diet plan, which is based on a book by the same name, claims that sugar is a deadly enemy and should be avoided. The plan calls for a zero-sugar, high-protein, low-carbohydrate diet. Yet many critics point out that sugar is not, in fact, naturally toxic. Furthermore, they argue, it is not a good idea to completely eliminate all sugar-containing foods, because some are good sources of energy, fiber, and other essential nutrients.

Difficulties and Dangers

Fad diets often do help people lose weight. The problem, however, is that the result is almost always temporary. Most people are terrible at keeping the lost weight off for the long-term. Several possible reasons lie behind this problem. First of all, fad diets often have complicated rules. It is easy to get frustrated quickly and quit. Also, people often lose a few pounds, decide that is good enough, and stop their diet. Then they regain the weight, perhaps adding even more weight, and end up back at the beginning or worse. This is the trap known as yo-yo dieting, which is very hard on the body and bad for a person's health. Furthermore, fad diets in which people eat the same foods over and over can be extremely boring. This boredom can easily result in failure to stick with the plan.

NUTRITION FACT

54 percent

Percentage of fast-food chains that make nutritional information available on their menus

There is a common belief that fad diets—even if they do not work in the long-term—are not harmful. On the contrary, fad diets can sometimes lead to serious health problems, especially if they are single-food diets that promote eating only one kind of food (such as restricting consumption to only grapefruit or vegetable soup, both popular fad diets at one time). No single food provides all of the vitamins, minerals, and other substances that the body needs for good health. Following a diet that ignores these requirements can lead to malnutrition.

Another danger is that weight can be lost too quickly with a fad diet. The National Consumers League, which supports research and education to consumers on a wide variety of topics, advises, "For most people, the goal is to lose about 1 to 2 pounds a week. You are more likely to keep weight off if you lose it slowly. Do not try to lose too much too fast (such as 10 pounds in a week)."[18]

Fasting

Many people choose to skip eating altogether for a few days as a way to lose weight in a hurry. Going on a short fast will indeed drop a few pounds. The problem is that a lot of the weight that is lost will be water, not fat. This lost pound-age will not stay off for the long-term. Madelyn Fernstrom, founder and director of the University of Pittsburgh Medical Center's Weight Loss Management Center, says, "The appeal is that [fasting] is quick, but it is quick fluid loss, not sub-stantial weight loss. If it's easy off, it will come back quickly [once the diet ends]."[19]

Portion Distortion

Over the past twenty years, average portion sizes have increased dramatically in the United States. This fact has changed what people think of as a "normal" portion at home, too. Below are some examples of how growing portions lead to increased calories.

Comparison of Portions and Calories Twenty Years Ago with Today

Food	Twenty Years Ago		Today	
	Portion	Calories	Portion	Calories
Bagel	3" diameter	140	6" diameter	350
Cheeseburger	1	333	1	590
Spaghetti with meatballs	1 cup sauce, 3 small meatballs	500	2 cups sauce, 3 large meatballs	1,020
Soda	6.5 ounces	82	20 ounces	250
Blueberry muffin	1.5 ounces	210	5 ounces	500

Taken from: U.S. Department of Health and Human Services, "Portion Distortion and Serving Size," www.nhlbi.nih.gov/health/public/heart/obesity/wecan/eat-right/distortion.htm.

To Wolf or Not to Wolf?

Many people think that they should eat as fast as possible because it burns more calories and will help them lose weight. In fact, quite the opposite might be true. Researchers at Osaka University in Osaka, Japan, published a study indicating that eating quickly can dramatically raise the risk of obesity. The reasons for this are not entirely clear. It is likely that one factor is simply that eating quickly does not give the body enough time to know when it has had enough, with overeating the result.

That said, the rate at which people eat has no effect on the calories taken in or burned off. The type and amount of food consumed is what affects weight. Plus, there is another downside to eating food too quickly: Wolfing food down can lead to stomachaches and indigestion because the digestive system has to work harder to absorb the food.

Research has shown that wolfing down food quickly can dramatically raise the risk of obesity.

Some health specialists advocate fasting as a way of cleansing the body. They believe that a short-term fast (one day or less) can help clear out toxins that build up during digestion. Most healthy people can tolerate a short-term fast like this, although weakness, nausea, headaches, and depression are sometimes side effects. Significant health problems, however, can develop with an extended fast. Fasting can lead to lowered blood sugar and lowered blood pressure, which can both lead to dizziness and even fainting. Another serious risk during an extended fast is losing important nutrients. An extended fast can also result in a buildup of chemicals called ketones. Ketones are fats that are partly broken down in the kidneys and liver. An excess of ketones is called ketosis. The condition causes all sorts of problems, including a huge strain on the kidneys and really terrible breath.

In general fad diets and fasting are not effective methods of weight control. An exception is vegetarianism, which, if properly guided, can be very effective for shedding pounds and a very healthy way overall to eat. Vegetarians were once mocked by the general public as being "health nuts." This is far less common now, and a meatless diet is no longer considered a strange eating plan. Finding the right diet is important not only for maintaining a healthy weight, but also for overall good health.

CHAPTER 5

Staying Healthy Through Better Eating

Society has known for thousands of years that disease and diet are strongly related. People sometimes use the expression, "You are what you eat." That might not literally be true, but there is, nonetheless, a direct link between the food that people consume and their general health. How people eat—the dietary choices they make—has a significant impact on their overall health.

In some cases food can actually be useful in the battle against certain diseases and disorders. Nutrition has clear, direct, and remarkable results on daily well-being. Furthermore, it can lower the risk of—or even play a role in preventing—both minor and life-threatening diseases and may even help lead to a longer life span.

Longevity

Recently, especially since the 1980s, there has been considerable research into ways to live longer, including so-called antiaging medicines. The first and best tool in the battle to live longer is for people to change their diets for the better. With the proper nutrition, it is now estimated that people could live to be as old as 130 years. Studies show that lifestyle changes that include dietary changes may actually help slow the aging process for many people.

Because chronic diseases are a major cause of death, people may have longer and healthier lives if they limit foods that increase disease risk. This includes foods high in cholesterol, saturated fat, trans fat, and sodium. At the same time, people need to watch their calorie intake and increase nutrient-rich foods that help lower the risk of disease.

A well-balanced diet includes a variety of nutrient-dense foods and enough fluids—particularly water. People should eat plenty of brightly colored vegetables and fruits, lean meats and other protein sources, and healthy fats. A healthy diet includes fruits and vegetables (canned or frozen), legumes, whole grain breads and cereals, and low-fat dairy products. Also important are fish, nuts, and tomatoes. Fish and nuts contain omega-3 fatty acids, which are believed to improve the amount of lipids (fat molecules) in the blood and contribute to increased cardiovascular health.

As people age, the nutritional value of their diet becomes more important. Several studies show that proper nutrition can help slow down the rate of decline in people's immune systems as they age. One study, by Bruno Lesourd and his fellow researchers at the Charles Foix Hospital in France, shows

Nutrition in the Fast Lane

With so many Americans carrying excess weight, it is important to know the nutritional value of commonly eaten foods. Below are the calorie, protein, fat, and sodium content of some popular fast foods.

Food	Calories	Protein (g)	Fat (g)	Sodium (mg)
Kentucky Fried Chicken Drumstick & Wing	390	29	27	1,169
McDonald's Big Mac	590	24	34	1,090
McDonald's Large Fries	540	8	26	350
Pizza Hut 2 Slices Cheese	480	12	20	1,300
Subway 6" Veggie Delite	200	7	23	500

Taken from: Riley Hospital for Children, "Adolescents: 12–21,"
http://rileychildrenshospital.com/parents-and-patients/caring-for-kids/adolescents.jsp.

that poor nutrition in the elderly contributes to a decline in their immune functions and increase rates of infection and cancer. Lesourd's study shows that people can benefit from proper choices in daily nutrition as they age.

Calorie Reduction

Studies also show that humans live longer and healthier lives when they restrict the number of calories they consume. A calorie-restricted diet is believed to help prevent oxidative damage. (Oxidative damage is caused by the natural process of oxygen causing the production of molecules called free radicals. If unchecked, research indicates that this can lead to Alzheimer's and other serious diseases.) Numerous studies over the years on rodents, beginning in the 1930s at Cornell University in New York, show that mice and rats put on a diet with 30 percent fewer calories lived up to 40 percent longer than a comparison group. Calorie-restricted mice are also able to avoid many of the usual degenerative diseases associated with aging. Researchers wanted to know if a calorie-restricted diet would have a similar effect in primates. So two long-term studies with rhesus monkeys were begun in the 1990s.

One of these studies, led by gerontologist Richard Weindruch of the University of Wisconsin–Madison, began in 2000 and involved a colony of seventy-six rhesus monkeys. Half the monkeys were allowed to eat as much as they wanted, and the other half were restricted to a diet with 30 percent fewer calories. The monkeys on the restricted diet were given vitamin and mineral supplements to ward off the possibility of malnutrition. The results of Weindruch's study, published in 2009, show that 63 percent of the calorie-restricted monkeys were still alive, compared to only 45 percent of the comparison group. Fourteen of the monkeys in the comparison group had died from age-related illnesses, such as cardiovascular disease and cancer, compared to only five of the calorie-restricted monkeys. And the restricted monkeys had a lower rate of deterioration of brain matter and muscles, two conditions also related to aging.

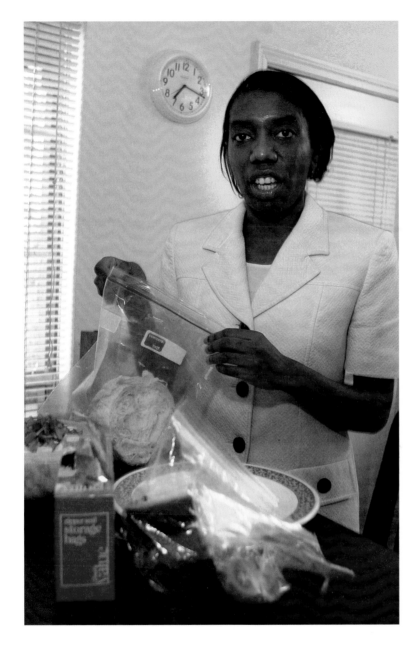

Kacy Collins prepares a low-calorie salad for lunch. She was a participant in the Pennington Biomedical Research Center study on the effects of restricted calories on longevity. She lost thirty pounds in the process.

The results of the study show that calorie restriction slows aging in primates, which may suggest that the same occurs in humans, but the only way to know is to conduct similar studies on humans. Long-term scientific studies of the effects of calorie restriction in humans, however, would take nearly a century to conduct, since people generally live much longer than monkeys. So far, research on humans has been confined to short-term studies.

While researchers do not know for sure that a calorie-restricted diet would give humans a longer life span, they have collected evidence that supports the theory. Luigi Fontana, an assistant professor of medicine at Washington University in St. Louis, Missouri, has conducted extensive research with a group called the Calorie Restriction Society. Members of this group follow a low-calorie, high-nutrition diet. In 2006 Fontana reported in the *Journal of the American College of Cardiology* that people who followed the calorie-restricted diet for an average of six years had hearts that appeared more elastic than those who did not follow a calorie-restricted diet. In addition, their hearts were able to relax between beats like the hearts of younger people.

In a study conducted at the Pennington Biomedical Research Center in Baton Rouge, Louisiana, researchers found that people who reduced their calories by 25 percent for a period of six months had less oxidative damage to their DNA, believed to be a sign of aging. One of the researchers, John O. Holloszy, says,

> This study has laid the groundwork for future research into the long-term effects of calorie restriction in humans. . . . It's going to be many years before we know whether calorie restriction really lengthens life, but if we can demonstrate that it changes these markers of aging, such as DNA damage and inflammation, we'll have a pretty good idea that it's somehow influencing the aging process at the cellular level.[20]

Obesity

Today more Americans are overweight than ever before. According to the American Obesity Association, 61 percent of the U.S. adult population is overweight, and 26 percent

---

NUTRITION FACT

1 in 6

Number of overweight adolescents in the United States with prediabetic symptoms

---

is obese. *Overweight* and *obese* are usually defined in terms of a person's body mass index (BMI). This is a measure of a person's weight in relation to height. A normal BMI is considered to be between 19 and 24.9. A person with a BMI between 25 and 30 is considered overweight, whereas a person with a BMI above 30 is considered obese. According to a CDC study released in 2010, overall obesity rates in America quadrupled between 1986 and 2000 and continue to rise. Furthermore, children are not immune from this trend. According to the CDC, obesity among American children aged six to eleven more than tripled, from 6.5 percent in 1980 to 19.6 percent in 2008.

Even more alarming than these statistics is the fact that carrying excess weight has been implicated in approximately three hundred thousand deaths a year. The location of the extra weight—in other words, where the fat is stored—can have an effect on a person's health. Having excess weight around the middle has been shown to have a direct association with an increased risk for heart disease. The risk for cancer increases with excess weight due to an elevation in

Having excess weight around the abdomen has been shown to increase the chances of heart disease and cancer.

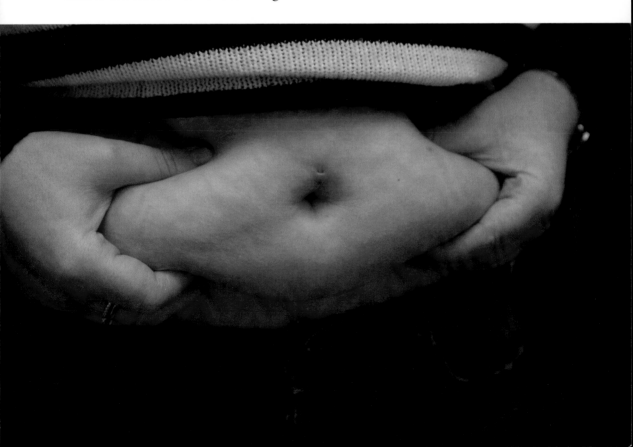

hormones; for example, estrogen, the female hormone, is synthesized in fat tissue, and elevated levels of estrogen are associated with cancers of the female reproductive system. In addition, being overweight or obese has been shown to be a risk factor for such serious maladies as high cholesterol, high blood pressure, digestive disorders, gallbladder complications, kidney disease, liver malfunction, stroke, and diabetes. Other complications that are linked to obesity include abdominal hernias, respiratory difficulties, sleep apnea, and varicose veins.

Preventing Disease with a Healthier Diet

A Mediterranean diet includes olive oil, fresh fruits and vegetables, beans, grains, nuts, fish, and shellfish but very little meat and poultry.

Obesity can be the result of overeating or following an unhealthy diet. A change to a healthier diet can go a long way in preventing many of the diseases associated with obesity. Jane E. Brody, a nutrition and personal health columnist for the *New York Times*, points out that in some ways, the typical American diet has improved in recent years. She says, "On average, we consume less red meat and saturated fat and somewhat more whole grains, fruits and vegetables. Our

processed foods were recently stripped of artery-clogging trans fats, thanks to a campaign that challenged the food industry to better protect American hearts."[21]

Yet even these improvements in eating habits are not enough to stem the obesity epidemic and the health issues associated with it. Brody explains:

> We are a long way from consuming the kind of diet most closely linked to a low risk of heart disease, cancer, diabetes, stroke and dementia. That diet need not be strictly vegetarian, but it should emphasize plant-based foods over the meat and other products that come from animals that eat plants. The closer to the earth we eat, the healthier—and leaner—we are likely to be.[22]

Many experts agree with Brody in advocating what is known as the Mediterranean diet. This pattern of eating takes its name from the part of the world where it is traditionally followed. The Mediterranean diet includes plenty of nutrient-rich fruits and vegetables, beans, grains, nuts, fish, and shellfish but little meat and poultry and low to moderate amounts of alcohol. It also includes plenty of olive oil as the main fat in cooking and eating.

Research published in 2009 on the *British Medical Journal*'s website supports the health benefits of the Mediterranean diet. Lead researcher Dimitrios Trichopoulos of the Harvard School of Public Health in Boston, Massachusetts, examined the eating habits of twenty-three thousand men and women for the study. He found that high consumption of vegetables and fruits, low intake of meat, and modest consumption of alcohol provided substantial health benefits. In addition, Trichopoulos says there are significant benefits when people combine several of the key components of the diet, such as high consumption of vegetables coupled with plenty of olive oil.

Brody sums up the health benefits of the Mediterranean diet: "This eating style, in its classic form, is most closely linked to a healthy body and mind as people age: a lower risk of heart disease, high blood pressure, stroke, diabetes, breast cancer and Alzheimer's disease."[23] She also points out that combining a healthy diet with regular physical activity is the key to maintaining a healthy weight and warding off the health risks associated with obesity.

Diabetes

Diabetes is among the disorders most commonly and most directly associated with obesity. In fact, diabetes is three times more likely in people with a BMI of 28 or higher. Diabetes is a serious condition that results when the body either cannot make enough insulin or its cells cannot absorb it. (Insulin is a hormone that helps the body use glucose.) There are two kinds of diabetes, known as type 1 and type 2. Type 2 diabetes is by far the more common and usually the less serious of the two. According to the National Institutes of Health, about 11 percent of U.S. adults, or 24 million people, have diabetes, and up to 95 percent of those have type 2 diabetes. If left untreated, diabetes can lead to a host of problems, including stroke; diseases of the kidneys, eyes, nervous system, and heart; as well as vascular disease so severe that amputation is sometimes necessary.

NUTRITION FACT

9

Number of calories per gram of fat

If diagnosed in time, however, type 2 diabetes can often be controlled through diet and exercise rather than medication. Yet its management through nutrition is not always obvious. Many people believe that someone who has diabetes, or wants to keep from getting it, needs to avoid candy and other refined sugars. This is not entirely true. Diabetics can ingest a small amount of sugar, but they need to monitor their total intake of carbohydrates and, to a lesser extent, fat and protein. According to the Mayo Clinic, diabetics need to make sure they eat a variety of healthy foods in moderate amounts and stick to a regular eating pattern in order to keep blood sugar levels stable.

The fact that diabetes is preventable through proper diet and exercise is demonstrated by a decade-long study involving thousands of people. The results of the Diabetes Prevention Program Outcomes Study were published in 2009

A Teen with Diabetes

Type 2 diabetes has been directly linked to obesity, and it is reaching alarming proportions in the United States. The other type of diabetes, type 1, typically occurs early in life. People who have either type must be very careful about what they eat. Here is what Erika, a teen who was twelve when she was diagnosed with type 1 diabetes, says about her eating habits:

> At breakfast I count carbohydrates and do some math in order to inject the proper dosage of insulin [her medication]. At lunch, dinner, and before bed it's the same routine. . . . It's not a good idea for me to skip meals. And I have the biggest sweet tooth imaginable. I mean I love candy (especially white chocolate) and ice cream. Before I was diagnosed with diabetes, I would eat it all the time. Afterward, well, let's just say I felt like a chronic smoker who had to stop smoking cold turkey. . . . Don't get me wrong, I am allowed to have sugar, as long as I don't go overboard. But let's be honest, once you have a slice, you want the whole cake.

Quoted in University of Minnesota Children's Hospital, "Diabetes: Erika's Story," http://universitychildrens.org/kidshealth/article.aspx?dn=uofmchildrenshospital &article_set=40766&lic=373&cat_id=20164.

in the British medical journal the *Lancet*. The study was a follow-up to an earlier study that included 3,234 people at high risk for diabetes. The two studies allowed researchers to look at the effects of lifestyle changes in preventing diabetes over the course of ten years. Researchers compared lifestyle changes designed to produce and maintain modest weight loss to taking an antidiabetic drug; both groups were compared to a control group that did not receive any treatment. The lifestyle changes included lowering the amount of fat and calories in the diet and increasing regular physical activity to 150 minutes a week.

Obesity and diabetes are directly linked, and it can be prevented by proper diet and exercise.

After ten years the rate of new diabetes cases developing in the lifestyle changes group was 34 percent lower than in the control group. For the antidiabetes drug group, the rate was 18 percent lower than in the control group. Looking at it another way, the lifestyle group delayed the onset of type 2 diabetes by about four years, and the drug group by about two years. This study showed that lifestyle changes had an even greater ability to prevent type 2 diabetes than drugs, thus highlighting the importance of diet and exercise in warding off diabetes.

Jill Crandall, an associate professor of clinical medicine at Albert Einstein College of Medicine of Yeshiva University, was a principal investigator in the Diabetes Prevention Program Outcomes Study. She says, "The group that had the most robust results from the lifestyle intervention was actually the older individuals, so that really should encourage people that it's never too late to begin these diabetes prevention efforts."[24]

Antioxidants and Cancer

Other diseases besides diabetes can also be prevented or minimized through proper eating. For example, eating foods rich in antioxidants may help in the prevention of cancer. Although it has not been definitively proved, research suggests that certain foods with antioxidants can be beneficial in lowering the risk of cancer. According to the University of Texas MD Anderson Cancer Center, "you can reduce your risk of cancer by as much as 30 to 40% by making healthier food choices. In fact, some foods can actually help protect against certain cancers."[25]

Blueberries, blackberries, raspberries, and strawberries are full of antioxidants and are believed to reduce oxidative damage and help prevent cancer.

Antioxidants are nutrients such as beta-carotene, selenium, lycopene, and vitamins A, C, and E. Fibrous foods, like vegetables and fruits, are good sources of antioxidants. These natural chemicals counter a process called oxidation, which is damage to body tissue that occurs either when the body breaks down food or through environmental factors such as tobacco smoke and radiation. Because this damage has been linked with increased cancer risk, antioxidants may play a role in lowering the risk of the disease. Berries, in particular, are a good choice, because the antioxidants in blueberries, blackberries, raspberries, and strawberries are believed to reduce oxidative damage and inflammation and promote cardiovascular and brain health in addition to helping prevent cancer.

Research shows that dietary factors play a significant role in fighting prostate cancer. In one study, mice that were fed a high-fat, high-cholesterol diet had an increased incidence of prostate tumor growth; furthermore, giving the mice a drug that blocks the absorption of cholesterol in the intestines prevented increased tumor growth. This suggests that reducing cholesterol levels in the diet may help prevent prostate cancer in humans. Another study found that restricting carbohydrate intake in mice could also help slow the growth of prostate tumors, and research is currently under way at Duke University in Durham, North Carolina, and the University of California–Los Angeles to determine whether restricting carbohydrates would produce a similar result in humans. Such a finding would be significant, because prostate cancer affects one in six men and is the most common form of cancer in men in the United States, after skin cancer.

Other dietary choices for preventing cancer include eating five to nine servings of fruits and vegetables a day. A low-fat diet is also essential, because high-fat diets are associated with certain types of cancer, including colorectal, prostate, and endometrial. Experts also recommend consuming low-fat or nonfat dairy products every day, because calcium may help protect against colorectal cancer. Because heavy drinking is associated with colon, breast, and liver cancer, alcohol should be consumed in moderation only or avoided altogether. Lastly, maintaining a healthy weight has been shown

Is Coffee Deadly?

It is a common myth that caffeine is a deadly poison. This would be true only if caffeine were taken in massive doses, and it is impossible to overdose on caffeine from coffee. It is estimated that a person would need to drink at least eighty cups of coffee, one right after another, to ingest a fatal dose.

Another myth is that coffee causes cancer. In the late 1970s and early 1980s, there was a lot of publicity over some studies that showed a possible link between coffee and certain cancers. Later research, however, indicates that there may be no connection, and in some cases, it may be just the opposite. A 2007 study in Japan found that drinking three or more cups of coffee a day would likely cut the risk of colon cancer in women by half. No change was found in the men studied.

A 2007 study in Japan found that drinking three or more cups of coffee per day could cut the risk of colon cancer in women by one-half.

to reduce the risk for many types of cancer, including breast, pancreatic, and kidney cancers.

Good nutrition and adequate exercise are the most important weapons in the battle against cancer and other diseases. As the MD Anderson Center explains, "Eating a plant-based, healthy diet (fruits, vegetables, whole grains and beans) and being physically active is your best insurance to reduce your risk of cancer, as well as heart disease and diabetes."[26] In addition, a healthy diet may be one of the best ways to ensure a longer and healthier life. Devising a well-balanced eating plan, and sticking with it, can dramatically and positively affect everyday life. After all, eating right is always an excellent idea.

NOTES

Chapter 1: Nutrition 101

1. Quoted in *NIH News in Health*, "Supplementing Your Diet: Vitamins, Minerals and Beyond," March 2006. http://newsinhealth.nih.gov/2006/March/docs/01features_01.htm.

Chapter 2: Nutrition and Metabolism

2. Lisa Balbach, "What Is Metabolism and Why Is It Important?" Health & Fitness Page. http://k2.kirtland.cc.mi.us/~balbachl/meta.htm.

3. Quoted in Colette Bouchez, "Make the Most of Your Metabolism," WebMD. www.webmd.com/fitness-exercise/guide/make-most-your-metabolism.

4. WebMD, "Slideshow: 10 Ways to Boost Your Metabolism." http://women.webmd.com/family-health-9/slideshow-boost-your-metabolism.

5. Go Ask Alice! "Is It Better to Eat Before or After Exercise?" January 7, 2005, www.goaskalice.columbia.edu/3306.html.

6. WebMD, "Slideshow."

7. HealthyNewAge.com, "Having Trouble Losing Weight? Natural Supplements to Boost Metabolism." www.healthynewage.com/Natural-Metabolism-Enhancer.html.

8. Quoted in Bouchez, "Make the Most of Your Metabolism."

9. U.S. Food and Drug Administration, "Tips for the Savvy Supplement User: Making Informed Decisions and Evaluating Information," January 2002. www.fda.gov/food/dietarysupplements/consumerinformation/ucm110567.htm.

Chapter 3: Nutrition and Exercise

10. Jane E. Brody, "Healthy Aging, with Nary a Supplement," *New York Times*, January 12, 2010. www.nytimes.com/2010/01/12/health/12brod.html?scp=17&sq=longevity&st=cse.

11. American College of Sports Medicine, "Physical Activity & Public Health Guidelines." www.acsm.org/AM/Template.cfm?Section=Home_

Page&TEMPLATE=CM/HTML
Display.cfm&CONTENTID=7764.

12. Charles Duhigg, "That Tap Water Is Legal but May Be Unhealthy," *New York Times*, December 16, 2009. www.nytimes.com/2009/12/17/us/17water.html.

13. Quoted in Anndee Hochman, "Top 6 Myths: About Bottled Water," WebMD. www.webmd.com/food-recipes/features/top-6-myths-about-bottled-water.

Chapter 4: Maintaining a Healthy Weight

14. Quoted in *Hartford (CT) Courant*, "10 Diet Myths Debunked." www.courant.com/health/sfl-tips-diet-myths-0121-pg,0,485303.photogallery?index=sfl-smheatdiet20090121104112.

15. National Heart, Lung and Blood Institute, "Fat-Free Versus Regular Calorie Comparison." www.nhlbi.nih.gov/health/public/heart/obesity/lose_wt/fat_free.htm.

16. Quoted in Margaret Wente, "Organic Tastes Good, but Better for Us? No," *Globe and Mail* (Toronto), July 10, 2009. www.theglobeandmail.com/news/opinions/organic-tastes-good-but-better-for-us-no/article1214614.

17. Quoted in Anushka Asthana and Rowan Walker, "Doctor to Expose 'Quick-Fix' Diet Myths," *New Zealand Herald*, November 23, 2009. www.nzherald.co.nz/news/print.cfm?objectid=10610958.

18. National Consumers League, "Safe Ways to Lose Weight." www.natlconsumersleague.org/obesity/weight_loss.htm.

19. Quoted in Susan Seliger, "Is Fasting Healthy?" WebMD. www.webmd.com/diet/features/is_fasting_healthy.

Chapter 5: Staying Healthy Through Better Eating

20. Quoted in *Science Daily*, "Thinner and Younger: Calorie Restriction Reduces Markers of Aging," April 5, 2006. www.sciencedaily.com/releases/2006/04/060405022759.htm.

21. Brody, "Healthy Aging, with Nary a Supplement."

22. Brody, "Healthy Aging, with Nary a Supplement."

23. Brody, "Healthy Aging, with Nary a Supplement."

24. Quoted in Albert Einstein College of Medicine of Yeshiva University, "Lifestyle Changes May Stave Off Diabetes for a Decade," November 2, 2009. www.einstein.yu.edu/home/news.asp?id=430.

25. University of Texas MD Anderson Cancer Center, "Diet & Nutrition." www.mdanderson.org/patient-and-cancer-information/cancer-information/cancer-topics/prevention-and-screening/diet-and-nutrition/index.html.

26. University of Texas MD Anderson Cancer Center, "Diet & Nutrition."

amino acids: The building blocks of proteins; these are used by the body to grow new tissue and to keep the brain and nervous system functioning properly.

antioxidant: A substance that reduces inflammation in the body.

calorie: A measure of how much energy the body gets from food.

carbohydrate: A substance found in foods, such as breads, rice, and potatoes, that provides energy for the body.

cholesterol: A waxy substance in the blood and cells of the body that helps to digest food, maintain cell membranes, and do other important jobs.

malnutrition: A harmful condition that can result from not eating enough food or from eating the wrong kinds of food.

metabolism: A measure of how the body converts food and other substances into fuel and how efficiently the body uses the energy that the fuel provides.

minerals: Inorganic substances, such as iron, zinc, and potassium, that are essential for good nutrition.

nutrients: Substances that provide elements that are essential for good health.

obese: Having a body mass index above 30; also defined as being 20 percent or more over ideal body weight.

overweight: Having a body mass index between 25 and 30; also defined as being up to 19 percent heavier than ideal body weight.

protein: A substance found in the cells of all living plants and animals. Meat, cheese, eggs, and beans are especially high in protein content.

vitamins: Organic substances that are found in foods and are essential to good health.

Centers for Disease Control and Prevention (CDC)

1600 Clifton Rd.
Atlanta, GA 30333
(800) 232-4636
e-mail: cdcinfo@cdc.gov
website: www.cdc.gov

The CDC is a branch of the U.S. Department of Health and Human Services. It is responsible for many areas of public health, including epidemic control, research, and nutrition information. Its website provides details on these and many more topics.

National Institutes of Health (NIH)

National Institutes of Health
9000 Rockville Pike
Bethesda, MD 20892
(301) 496-4000
website: www.nih.gov

The NIH is a branch of the U.S. Department of Health and Human Services. Its primary function is to conduct and support medical research. Its website provides a wide range of information, including detailed sections on topics targeting teen health.

U.S. Department of Agriculture (USDA)

3101 Park Center Dr., Rm. 1034
Alexandria, VA 22302

(888) 779-7264
e-mail: support@cnpp.usda.gov
website: www.mypyramid.gov

The USDA is the organization within the U.S. government that (among its many other responsibilities) sets the standards for the MyPyramid nutritional guidelines. Its website has a lot of information for people of all ages, including a wide range of resources.

U.S. Department of Health and Human Services

200 Independence Ave. SW
Washington, DC 20201
(877) 696-6775
website: www.hhs.gov

This is the U.S. government's chief department for providing social services regarding health issues, including programs in nutrition education, substance abuse treatment, regulation of some aspects of food safety, and health information for mothers and children. Its website provides detailed information on these and many other topics as well as a link to one of its subsidiary organizations, FoodSafety.gov, that specifically targets food and nutrition.

Books

Robin Brancato, *Food Choices: The Ultimate Teen Guide*. Lanham, MD: Scarecrow, 2010. This book focuses, in part, on the biological and chemical reasons behind the food preferences of teens.

Rozanne Gold and Helen Kimmel, *Eat Fresh Food: Awesome Recipes for Teen Chefs*. New York: Bloomsbury, 2009. This book, cowritten by an award-winning food writer and a nutritionist, is fun to use.

Christopher Hovius, *The Best You Can Be: A Teen's Guide to Fitness and Nutrition*. Broomall, PA: Mason Crest, 2005. This is a well-written introduction to the subject.

Michael Pollan, *The Omnivore's Dilemma for Kids*. New York: Dial, 2009. Written for kids, this book discusses the paths food takes before being consumed.

Donna Shryer, *Body Fuel: A Guide to Good Nutrition*. Tarrytown, NY: Marshall Cavendish, 2008. This is an excellent guide to a complex topic.

Internet Sources

American Cancer Society, "Common Questions About Diet and Cancer," www.cancer.org/healthy/eathealthyg etactive/acsguidelinesonnutrition physicalactivityforcancerprevention/ acs-guidelines-on-nutrition-and-physical-activity-for-cancer-preven tion-diet-cancer-questions.

KidsHealth, "The Food Guide Pyramid," http://kidshealth.org/kid/stay_ healthy/food/pyramid.html.

Websites

BAM! Body and Mind (www.bam.gov). This site, maintained by the Centers for Disease Control and Prevention, is designed especially for young adults.

MyPyramid.gov (www.mypyramid .gov). This website, managed by the U.S. Department of Agriculture, offers extensive information on healthy eating and exercise.

Nutrition.gov (www.nutrition.gov). This is the main site for the U.S. Department of Agriculture's Nutritional Information Service. It is a gateway to many groups within the federal government that deal with food safety and education. In addition, it provides a wide range of material (including downloadable information) on such topics as food safety in the home, current poisoning outbreaks, product recalls, and industry inspection guidelines.

SNAC (www.snac.ucla.edu). This site is maintained by the Student Nutrition (and Body Image) Action Committee at the University of California–Los Angeles. This site covers many topics, including how spirituality and emotions relate to nutrition for young adults.

U.S. Department of Health and Human Services (www.health.gov). This is the official website of the government department concerned with health issues. The site provides "Physical Activity Guidelines for Americans" as well as "Dietary Guidelines for Americans." It contains complete information about its official guidelines for nutrition and offers

Salt, 14

Scurvy, 21

Serving size. *See* Portion/serving
  size

Sleepiness, 35

Sleeping Beauty diet, 61

Snacks/snacking
  benefits of, 32–34
  salads for weight loss and,
    55–56

Sodium, 47, 49

Soft drinks, 42

Sports drinks, 44–47

SportsMed (Web site), 50

Starchy foods, 54

Sugar Busters! diet, 62

Sugars, 47

Supplements, 34, 36–37

T

Trans fats, 17

Trichopoulos, Dimitrios,
  73

Turkey, L-tryptophan in,
  35

U

United States
  obesity rates, 71
  soft drink consumption
    per person, 42

University of Texas MD Anderson
  Cancer Center, 77, 80

V

Vegetables, 12
  raw, 58
  as source of antioxidants,
    78
  weight loss and, 55–56

Vegetarianism, 52, 57, 65

Vitamin A, 20
  overdose of, 22–23
  sources of, 12

Vitamin B, 21

Vitamin C, 21

Vitamin D, 19, 21

Vitamin K, 21

Vitamins
  fat soluble *vs.* water soluble,
    21–23
  in sports drinks, 46
  vegetarian sources of, 59

W

Water
  bottled *vs.* tap, 42–44
  importance of, during
    exercise, 41–42
  metabolism and, 26

WebMD (website), 26, 27,
  32

PICTURE CREDITS

ABOUT THE AUTHOR

Adam Woog has written many books for children, young adults, and adults. He lives in Seattle, Washington, with his wife. They have one daughter. The author dedicates this book to M., who saved his soy-based bacon.